How To GRASP Confidence & Own Your Power

Become the Most Confident Version of Yourself in 5 simple steps

By: Tara LaFon Gooch, MBA

Copyright © 2023 Tara LaFon Gooch, MBA All rights reserved

No part of this book may be reproduced, or stored in a retrieval system, or transmitted in any form or by any means, electronic, mechanical, photocopying, recording, or otherwise, without express written permission of the publisher.

ISBN: 9798856248875

"When I dare to be powerful, to use my strength in the service of my vision, then it becomes less and less important whether I am afraid." - Audre Lorde

Contents

Title Page

Copyright

Epigraph

Dedication

Foreword

Chapter 1: Gratitude for the Person You Were   1

Chapter 2: Gratitude for the Person You Are   50

Chapter 3: Gratitude for the Person You Are Becoming   78

Chapter 4: Responsibility   105

Chapter 5: Action   128

Chapter 6: Sight   148

Chapter 7: Purpose: Where to Start   165

Chapter 8: Purpose: Identifying Your Core Values   211

Conclusion   252

About the Author   262

Special Acknowledgements   264

Citations   267

Endorsements

"From the moment I met Tara, my life took an extraordinary turn, and in the briefest of encounters, she left an indelible mark on my soul. What intrigued me most about her was the humble, yet astounding power she effortlessly embodied. As I immersed myself in the pages of her book, "How to GRASP Confidence and Own Your Power," I was captivated by the same unique qualities that had drawn me to her in person. Tara's writing offers a refreshingly simplistic approach that yields profound results, setting it apart from the myriad self-help books I had come across in the past.

Unyielding in her candor, Tara fearlessly bares her vulnerabilities and recounts the hurdles she faced from her formative years into adulthood. This genuine openness forged a deep and resonating connection, leaving me feeling understood and empowered. It became evident that I, too, possessed the potential to reshape my life, armed with the simple yet potent tools she offers to her readers. Tara's journey exemplifies how even those of us who feel we have nothing to offer can make a significant impact simply by shifting our perspective on our own innate values. Her no-nonsense approach to achieving success presents a clear and easy-to-follow step-by-step process that anyone can adopt, utilizing gratitude and their own God-given gifts to carve a path straight to the top.

In a time when I found myself slipping into a disheartening rut, Tara's book came into my life as a beacon of hope and inspiration. Amidst my self-doubt, her story reminded me that failures do not define us and that there is immense potential within us to achieve greatness. She proved to be the encouraging mentor I needed to regain confidence and believe in my ability to shine brightly.

As I look back on the chapters she penned, I eagerly anticipate revisiting them whenever I feel myself veering off course. Tara's book is more than just a read; it is a guiding light that provides hope and clarity during life's rough patches. We could all benefit from having a Tara in our lives—someone who uplifts and empowers us, reminding us of our boundless potential.

I can hardly wait to turn to Tara's words whenever I need

a boost, reminding myself of the strength I possess to stay on the right path and achieve my dreams. "How to GRASP Confidence and Own Your Power" is a true gem that will continue to inspire and motivate me whenever life's challenges threaten to dim my shine."

SOTERIA KONTIS,

AUTHOR & SPEAKER

"Tara's GRASP method is a simple, five step process that is guaranteed to bring you to the next level. Confidence is a superpower that unlocks everything in your life. Do yourself a favor and grab a copy of this book today! You'll be so glad you did!"

DR. STEPHANIE STODDART MBA,

DENTIST & COACH

"Tara Gooch writes a compelling and insightful book on the transformational power for owning confidence. She uses her own experiences and anecdotes to fully express the importance of confidence and how it will change every area of your life. If you want one book to level up your game, this is it. Well done, Tara!"

CINDI COHN,

BEST SELLING AUTHOR, TV PERSONALITY, & COACH

"This book gave me gold nuggets in every chapter and lead me to deep introspection. The methods taught allowed me to learn how to reengineer my thought process to become more confident. I also learned how to accept my past and move forward to my present. Each chapter made me reflect on how I want to empower my child to become gracious, compassionated, and more confident with his decision-making process.

Tara you are masterful in convening how to build upon your struggles to become a better version of yourself with authentic happiness and sense of accomplishment. I recommend this book, if you would like to work on step-by-step plan to learn and practice confidence every day of your life."

LINA ECHEVERRY-HART,

BUSINESS STRATEGIST & CONSULTANT

"Tara takes you on a journey through a difficult childhood that could have easily resulted in an adult life of mere survival. Instead, she found her purpose through developing her confidence. These are life skills, that, if practiced consistently, can change your whole outlook and world view. Your true purpose is already inside you. This book can help you uncover it."

LEAH NEAL,

PERSONAL BRANDING COACH

"What if your brand is the story of how you turned your heartbreaks and struggles into living a bolder, bigger, and fuller life? That's the premise of Tara LaFon Gooch's book, "How To GRASP Confidence & Own Your Power." I began reading the book between meetings and could not put it down. This is a "mind-shifting" book. The book flows smoothly, like a conversation with a wise and trusted friend, with powerful life stories and observations, this book is very relatable and practical, as the author has actually lived and achieved confidence and success through the methods she teaches in this book. Through the GRASP framework, Gratitude, Responsibility, Action, Sight, and finally, Purpose, Tara guides you step by step to define what is needed to lead a more fulfilled, confident, and purposeful life. This is a book that I will recommend to my clients and team members."

DR. ARDESHIR MEHRAN, PH.D.,

BEST SELLING AUTHOR & FOUNDER, HUMAN WORK STUDIO

"Gratitude is one of the foundations for leading a life of abundance. Expressing gratitude daily is crucial to raising your vibration which ultimately leads to taking action that you ordinarily would not take. This in turn, this leads to exteriority results! Two words - Massive Action. Thank you for bringing this book to the world and helping others build confidence with a foundation of gratitude."

GARY B. DOHERTY,

CEO OF THINK NETWORK &

CEO BE SEEN PR AGENCY

"I just finished Tara's book as well as her book club. There is so much power packed into both. Tara knows from whence she speaks and writes sharing her own story beautifully and vulnerably. I learned so much from the book about how I approach my life. One of my favorite lines "you are not a victim on your circumstances, you are a product of your actions." Tara walks the walk, and you will learn and grow from the life-changing, powerhouse of a human. Read this book!"

DONNA STAR,

EXECUTIVE COACH, BUSINESS CONSULTANT, & AUTHOR

"From the moment she entered my life, Tara has been the embodiment of the words that guided her from her lowest point into the life force she has become: "Give more." And now, in her book, Tara gives her all by pouring her heart and soul into her message of inspiring us to empower ourselves. She teaches by example, showing rather than telling her readers by selflessly drawing back the curtain on her own struggles, obstacles, and setbacks. Despite having been victimized for much of her life, Tara is no victim - her no-nonsense authentic voice shines through with a strength that says - "You Can Do This!" And that she has. I have no doubt this book will inspire and motivate many to find their power and put it into action, as it has for me."

LONICA SMITH, ESQ.,

ATTORNEY & HUMAN RIGHTS ADVOCATE

"This is by far one of the best books I have read on confidence. The GRASP method is not only empowering and uplifting, but powerful and transformative. Thank you, Tara for sharing this amazing story, and taking us on this amazing journey that teaches us despite the challenges and pitfalls we face in life, we can all rise high on the wings of confidence!"

MITZIE WILLIAMS,

8X PUBLISHED AUTHOR, ATTORNEY, UNIVERSITY

LECTURER, COURSE CREATOR, TEDX ORGANIZER,

PROFESSIONAL SPEAKING COACH, AUTHOR & CREATOR OF

THE "DRAWING FROM YOUR WELL" SERIES

Dedication

This book is dedicated to my daughter, Nora. From the moment I first laid my eyes on you, I loved you. You made me a mother; you believed in me even when I didn't believe in myself, and through your love I realized that I was worthy and deserving of more. I could not ask for a more beautiful, smart, loving, and confident daughter.

Foreword

You were born confident, we all were. No baby has ever been born believing it is unworthy or undeserving of its parents' attention. Babies cry and are confident in their abilities to have their needs met. As toddlers, we learn how to walk, eat, talk, and do things independently; all of which work to build levels of confidence within us. A toddler when learning how to walk does not fall and then believe they are a failure, the young child thinks nothing of the sort. They simply get back up and keep going, they are innately confident. Even though they are beginners they do not believe they are failing, and they remain confident that eventually they will understand how to walk, run, jump, and play sports. As John Lennon once said, "Every child is an artist until he's told he's not an artist." The same can be said about confidence, every child is confident until someone or something brings them down. Gradually as we encounter life's obstacles, perceived failures, hardships, and traumas our confidence begins to dissipate and diminish. Confidence can begin to seem elusive and untouchable for many people as they enter adulthood and proceed in their careers. Throughout our adult lives we face barriers that all work to lessen our confidence and it can be difficult to overcome for many people, especially for those who have lived through trauma, adversity, and hardship. Sadly, a lack of confidence holds many people back in life, preventing them from tapping into their fullest potential, becoming successful, and feeling purposeful.

Even though confidence can begin to lessen over the course of our lives, it is possible to regain it. Ultimately, while some individuals may be naturally more confident than others, confidence is a skill that can be learned, cultivated, and developed through intentional effort and practice. This book will take you on my journey from unconfident and aimless to confident, successful, purpose-driven and inspired. My journey to becoming my most confident self was not an overnight manifestation but the lessons I learned along the way helped shape me into the person I am today and for that I am forever grateful. My sincere hope is that this book helps anyone who is struggling with confidence realize that your life begins the moment you step into the confident person you are meant to be, and that person is already exists within you. Confidence is not just a state of mind; it's the fuel that propels dreams into reality, transforms doubt into determination, and turns setbacks into stepping stones.

There is no room for masks, false bravado, or pretense in this book, I openly share my story and my journey with you so that you can have the tools to live your best life. My intention is to lead by example and show you what's possible for you to achieve in a short amount of time based on my personal experience. Through my 5-step GRASP method, you will learn to cultivate gratitude, shoulder responsibility, take action, achieve sight, and align with your purpose.

The GRASP method saved my life and helped me go from feeling unloved, depressed, anxious, suicidal, and purposeless to feeling highly confident, driven, and inspired in only a few short months. My goal is to help every reader understand that no matter your hurt, struggle, or pain, you can go on to live a better life filled with increased confidence. However, you must put in the work, and it takes daily action and progress in the right direction with a growth-oriented mindset to fully step into the best, most confident version of yourself. If you are fully committed to that process and are willing to put in the work, keep reading.

This book is based upon my own journey and experiences and was written to be easily understood and actionable. My intention is to provide anyone reading this book with the tools to build confidence, regardless of their past or present circumstances. It is my firm belief that we can each gain and develop confidence and my hope is that anyone reading this book share the methods and concepts taught with someone else and pay it forward. Confidence is often a silent struggle that many are facing but are afraid to admit. Through teaching this method you not only learn the method deeper and with a greater sense of clarity and appreciation, but you also empower another individual with life-changing information. We never know what someone else has gone through or is going through so pay it forward by providing someone else with the tools needed to be confident and live their best life.

5 Step Method To
GRASP CONFIDENCE

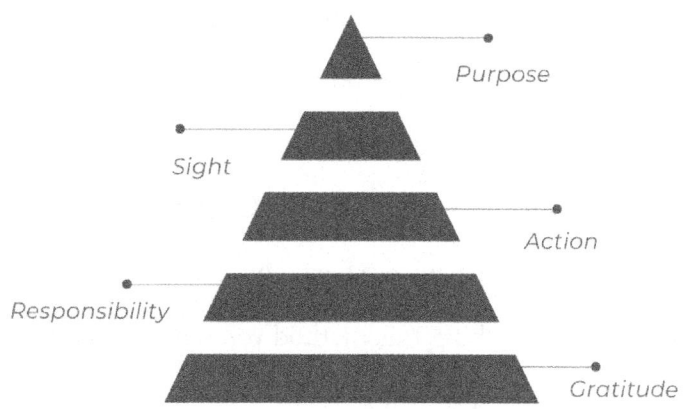

- Purpose
- Sight
- Action
- Responsibility
- Gratitude

© TARA LAFON GOOCH

Chapter 1: Gratitude for the Person You Were

With a bottle of Benadryl in hand and my plan set I looked out of my bedroom window at the blue sky for what I thought would be the last time. Between past childhood trauma that went unresolved, general unfulfillment with my life, toxic workplaces, and feeling as though I didn't have a friend in the world to lean on, I became convinced that I needed to end my life and on March 16, 2022, I almost did. I remember it clearly; it was an incredibly beautiful spring day in North Carolina where I live. My mind was made up, and I was going to go through with ending my life. I was going to turn on my car, let the exhaust fill up the garage, close the door and all the windows, take my Benadryl, and never wake up again.

Before I took the Benadryl, I decided to pray one last time to anything or anyone that could hear me if anyone existed or cared. I looked out of my bedroom window,

Benadryl in hand and looked at the sky. I screamed out loud to the top of my lungs and said, "If there is a God who gives a damn tell me why I am here, what is my purpose?" I remember shaking I was crying so hard. I looked up at the blue sky. I yelled these words repeatedly, and finally, out of exhaustion, I stopped screaming and started listening. The words that came into my mind were as clear as someone talking directly into my ear, and they confused me at first. I didn't understand the message. The words I heard were, "Your life has meaning, but you need to give more." Then, I kept hearing the words "give more," "give more," "give more." It provided the needed distraction to prevent the act of suicide. The words "give more" saved my life. Over the next few days, I contemplated in my mind what "give more" meant. What could I possibly give to anyone, what value did I have – until I realized a profound and universal truth, we all have more to give than we can even begin to realize.

Over the next several weeks and months, I began by giving more of myself to others, even if it was the giving of my time to help someone else. When I began my journey of giving, I had a relatively large LinkedIn network and while

I hadn't gotten to know anyone personally yet, I started reaching out to people who seemed like-minded, who were kind, positive, and looking to grow in their own ways and I started paying attention. I wanted to find my tribe and I sought out supportive people who I could help but who in turn could also help me. I began posting positive content to find other people who shared the same values and when I found them, I would connect with them and support them. What started out as trying to "give more" to an online community turned into several networking opportunities and even business partnerships. I had no idea how naturally talented I was at networking until I started giving and reaching out to people and I was truly surprised by the results of my efforts. I was able to connect with high-powered executives, industry leaders, best-selling authors, and successful entrepreneurs from all over the globe in a short amount of time. I joined several networking groups and eventually this led me to accepting a role as the United States Country Chair for a global women's leadership league. I began helping female entrepreneurs and startup companies launch and scale their businesses and develop strategies that led them to becoming successful. All of which helped develop my confidence, but it also built very powerful alliances that helped propel my career and the level of self-belief that I had.

I helped several professionals within my social network find jobs and pivot successfully in their careers and over time I started to realize how many skills I had and how valuable I was to other people. I performed smaller acts of service as well and assisted local neighbors by cooking them a meal or taking care of a chore for them. These small acts of giving had a profound impact on my self-confidence, and I started to find fulfillment for the first time in my life. I went from being a burnout corporate sales executive feeling as though I had no purpose in the world to purposeful beyond measure simply by giving. I practiced small acts of giving that eventually became progressively larger and more generous. At the grocery story I would pay for the person ahead of me in line or pay for the person behind me while ordering at a restaurant. Even though these were small acts I could feel them changing me. Soon these small acts of giving resulted in larger acts of generosity and I decided to help thirty-six professionals from all over the globe develop an effective content strategy, teach them how to network professionally, build their personal brands, and an online presence on LinkedIn to help propel their careers. This led to me receiving many positive reviews for my business as well as forming relationships with many amazing people. It is simply incredible to reflect on how much global impact I had in a short amount of time simply by realizing that I had skills and talents that were useful to other people and in demand. I learned this all by giving.

I realized that to do more and be more, I needed to give more. When you approach any situation in life or in business with the attitude of giving, it will result in growth because it creates impact both within yourself and with the world around you. Everyone that interacts with you feels the gratitude and the generosity that you radiate and as a result, everyone benefits and is made better simply through by interacting with you. For so many years of my life I wasn't grateful because I wasn't truly giving, I didn't realize how many skills and talents I had. Not only was I doing myself a disservice, but the entire world. Giving changed me, it opened my heart, and it brought me closer to God. I encourage everyone reading this book to give more to someone in need today, you never know how much impact even a small act of service can have on that other person's life, but yours as well.

When you give to someone else it creates gratitude within the other individual but also within yourself. You realize how much abundance you have, and it allows you to become more present-minded and joyful, and that joy is contagious. What started as small pay-it-forward acts of service led to larger audiences online. I began coaching individuals and groups how to develop successful personal brands for themselves, how to show up effectively online, the basics of social networking, as well as how to produce content that helped them reach their professional goals. All of these were natural skills that I possessed and by helping other people overcome their limitations, it helped me gain confidence in my abilities.

I went on a mission to help support others by giving them opportunities for success and confidence. What started out as a voice in my head that told me to "give more" became a movement and mission to create global impact through acts of service and gratitude.

Many religious and spiritual traditions emphasize the importance of giving as a means of developing a deeper understanding of God or the divine. When we give to others, we are showing kindness and concern for their well-being, which can be seen as an act of love towards all of God's creation. Moreover, giving can also be a way of expressing gratitude for the blessings one has received in life. This can foster a sense of humility and appreciation for the goodness in the world, which may help individuals to connect with the divine. When we are grateful for what we have, we are more likely to recognize the blessings in our lives and see them as gifts from a loving God. There is no God that exists that wants less for you and more for someone else. God wants good things for all. When you give, you get closer to understanding how we are all connected and what it means to love. By serving others, it is possible to develop a deeper understanding of the interconnectedness of all beings and the importance of working towards the greater good. When we serve others, we are not only helping them, but we are also contributing to a better world and fulfilling a higher purpose. You become closer to the creative forces all around you and within you. It feels like a metamorphosis and awakening.

Giving can also be a way of practicing detachment from material possessions and attachments. This can help individuals cultivate a more spiritual perspective on life and focus on what is truly important. When we let go of our attachments to material things, we free ourselves from the distractions of the world and can focus more fully on our spiritual growth and development. Overall, giving can be a powerful spiritual practice that helps individuals to connect with the divine, develop virtues like generosity and compassion, and cultivate a deeper sense of purpose and meaning in life. Giving fosters gratitude and builds confidence. Giving made me realize I was talented and helped me see how many skills I possessed that were helpful to others. Giving helped launch my business and it made me a purpose-driven entrepreneur on a mission to create global impact.

No matter how low you are feeling, no matter how worthless you believe yourself to be, no matter how depressed or anxious you feel, or no matter how little you think you have -- when you give, it will lead you to gratitude. Gratitude is powerful because it can help you to align with your purpose and greater calling in life. Gratitude is a high vibration energy; it carries a positive and uplifting frequency. In terms of energy and vibrations, everything in the universe is believed to have its own energetic frequency. Higher vibrational energies are associated with positive emotions, abundance, love, and joy, while lower vibrational energies are linked to negative emotions such as fear, anger, and sadness. In essence, the concept of gratitude as a high vibrational energy suggests that by cultivating a grateful mindset and expressing gratitude regularly, we can elevate our own energy and attract more positive experiences and manifestations into our lives. It is a way of aligning ourselves with the abundance and positivity that already exists in the world around us. Gratitude is undoubtedly transformative and has the power and potential to change your life, increase your confidence, help you heal, and bring you closer to the universal energy that binds all things.

 The best and most effective way to develop a present

minded state is to be grateful and to think about things you are grateful for in your life. To align with your purpose and why you were put on this Earth, you must be present minded. You cannot be focused on the past or future to find your purpose, you must be aligned with your present mind, and you do this by practicing gratitude.

The words "give more" saved my life and they can save yours as well. My story is proof that no matter how low you feel or what happened to you in your past, when you give it starts a chain of events to occur that will change your life forever.

Gratitude For the Person I Was

I am the youngest child of five from a single mother, and I haven't seen my father since I was fourteen years old after my parents divorced. I grew up in a home that had unfinished construction and was in many ways in shambles. We lived in the middle of the woods in rural Maryland by a river and had few neighbors. Prior to my birth, my family's home did not have running water or indoor plumbing, and we had an outhouse instead of a bathroom. Our home did not have traditional heating, we had a wood stove which was minimally functional and never seemed to heat our home enough, especially during bitterly cold months. It is incredible to think how poor we were. The county we lived in was one of the richest counties in the United States, yet I grew up in poverty. Even though we had little means monetarily, we had a large garden which helped my mother to be able to feed our family on her salary as a housekeeper.

I learned self-sufficiency at a very young age. I would load the wood stove to heat the home, help my mother can goods and cook meals. I learned as a child how to feed a family with minimal resources. We frequently ate soup because soup could feed many people and the ingredients could be sourced from our land. My father had a felony record and was an alcoholic. He was mentally, physically, and emotionally abusive to my mother, myself, and my siblings growing up. He couldn't hold a steady job, which contributed to our family's financial situation. He had talents in carpentry and construction, but nothing was ever finished, including our home. He was a junk collector and hoarder and rarely threw anything away. If a car became unusable it would just get added to the stockpile of other cars on our property until there were as many as twenty useless, inoperable vehicles in our yard. Our home looked like junk and we were surrounded by junk. He would rarely mow our land, it was unkempt, unattractive and as a child I was embarrassed by it.

The things we witness, experience, and go through in our lives can impact our ability to be confident. This is especially true if you grow up in fear, lived through trauma, experienced poverty, suffered abuse, or have one or more drug or alcohol dependent parents. When a child lives in fight or flight mode, it works to change the physiology of developing brains. "Early exposure to trauma — extremely fearful events — and high levels of stress affect the developing brain, particularly in those areas involved in emotions and learning" (National Scientific Council on the Developing Child, 2010).

Perhaps it was a traumatic experience or event, it could have even been a series of negative experiences or your environment which began to chip away at our confidence. Have you ever thought about when or at what point in your life you started feeling unconfident, ashamed, or even fearful?

When I was about eight years old, my father, mother, and elder brother were at my dad's cousin's home. We stayed there for several hours, and my brother and I mostly spent time outside playing and running around while the adults stayed inside drinking White Russians. It was dark when we left. I remember sitting in the backseat of our black Chevy Impala holding my older brother's hand as we both cried on the way home because we weren't sure we were going to make it back alive. My father was swerving all over the road and I remember telling my older brother how scared I was, we held each other's hands and I remember praying to God to help us. On the drive home, we just missed hitting an oncoming semitruck and dodged a large tree in a curve of the road. Even though my older brother was usually tough, I could see the fear in his eyes as we drove home that night. I will never forget how close we came to not getting home that night. When you live in fear and are unsafe it can make you believe that the situations you are experiencing, you are deserving of and overtime your confidence begins to diminish and become seemingly unreachable.

A lack of confidence doesn't surface overnight, generally feelings of inadequacy often begin in childhood. As someone who grew up in less than favorable circumstances, it is understandable how I suffered from a lack of confidence into my adult life. During therapy I had several revelations about my childhood and the origin of my lack of confidence along with the feeling that I didn't have a voice. These revelations helped me develop a deep understanding of patterns and behaviors that I was continuing to experience in my life and allowed me to understand that I was going through a cycle and how to break the cycle.

Prior to therapy I had never considered that a lack of confidence could be a generational cycle and pattern. I had believed that my confidence was due to my childhood circumstances and while that was part of it, I began to also see that it was a learned behavior. I had learned a lack of confidence from my mother. I saw her mentally, emotionally, and physically abused by my father and as a result she was powerfully unconfident. Her mannerisms were unconfident, her body language was unconfident, the way she spoke about herself was unconfident, she never stood up for herself, she over apologized for everything, and she continually put everyone else's needs above her own. I was unintentionally modeling this behavior and adapting it as my own.

Children learn, mimic, and imitate their parents and environment and during therapy I came to the realization that my lack of confidence was a learned behavior. Children observe and learn from their parents' behavior, including their levels of confidence. If parents consistently display self-doubt, lack of assertiveness, or low self-esteem, children may internalize these attitudes and behaviors as normal. They may learn to doubt their own abilities, hesitate to take risks, or struggle with asserting themselves. Emotional support and validation from parents are crucial for building children's confidence and when children don't have this it can lead them to repeating the cycle. When parents fail to provide encouragement, praise, or emotional support, children may feel unacknowledged and develop a sense of insecurity and self-doubt. In my case, I had never experienced love, emotional connection, or support whatsoever from my father. Between the lack of stability at home, financial insecurities, uncertainty, and a lack of representation of what confidence looked like, I was unconsciously exhibiting the same behavior. I realized that I needed to make a change for myself and for my young daughter. The last thing I wanted was for her to learn and model my lack of confidence and grow up doubting herself and suffering as I did. I knew she deserved more but I had to show her through my actions and lead by example to break the cycle once and for all.

Growing up in poverty or in low-income environments can have a range of negative effects on a child's physical, emotional, and cognitive development. According to research from JAMA Pediatrics, "On average, children from low-income households scored 4 to 7 points lower on standardized tests ($P < .05$). As much as 20% of the gap in test scores could be explained by maturational lags in the frontal and temporal lobes" (Hair, et al., 2015). The impact that poverty and abuse can have on children can diminish future opportunities for success and if left unaddressed can lead to a continuation of the cycle. As a child who experienced abuse and trauma at home, I remember feeling anxious, isolated, and disconnected from others, which caused me to struggle with social interactions in academic settings. For many years, I struggled to trust others, had difficulty forming relationships, and felt ashamed and embarrassed about my home life. Abusive home environments often involve a great deal of control and power dynamics, which often made me feel powerless and unable to assert myself. I learned to avoid confrontation, stay silent, and to comply with authority figures to avoid triggering anger or retaliation.

I withdrew from my life and into myself. My home life weighed on me, it made me feel inferior and as if I was incomplete, unworthy, and dysfunctional. I was always looking for ways to escape my circumstances. At home, I had the woods to escape to when I wanted to get away. The adventures I went on as I wondered the woods were happy memories. We had a river near our home, and I would often go there with my dogs to play in nature and escape from my circumstances. Nature has always been a sanctuary for me and somewhere I felt at peace. At school, escape was more difficult. My shame and withdrawal made it difficult to connect with other kids, and I was often bullied and teased in school. I frequently sat alone at lunch, I was never once asked to a school dance, I was endlessly picked on, and I never had the confidence to stand up for myself. I struggled with reading, spelling, and math and was incorrectly diagnosed with a learning disability in elementary school. As a result, I was put on medication and placed in remedial classes from elementary school until High School which worked to lessen my self-esteem and erased what was left of my confidence and self-worth. I was terrified to raise my voice in class. I would never raise my hand; I would dread presenting in front of my class, and I would sit in the back of the class and try to be unseen in every possible way.

During Elementary school I recall my teacher instructing the class to sit in a circle and for each of us to read a line from a book. I would busily read and try to memorize my line so that I wouldn't fail when it was my turn to speak. This led me to not being able to capture the full story of the book because I was more focused on not messing up, being picked on, or failing than I was learning. My voice would crack, my head would be down, my face would turn red, and my eyes would well up with tears if I had to speak and on more than one occasion it led to me running to the bathroom to cry. I was so powerfully unconfident that the thought of someone seeing or hearing me was enough to terrify me.

It wasn't until my sophomore year in high school, when an English teacher told me that a paper, I wrote was the best submission in the class, that I felt someone believed in me, my abilities, and what I was capable of. I didn't know it at the time but this teacher who believed in me helped me to see that I had talents and value and for the first time in school I felt smart and capable. My paper described the struggle, trials, and tribulations of *The Crucible's* main character, John Proctor, and how he had felt forsaken by his neighbors, family, church, and friends during the Salem Witch trials. My paper was well-written because even at the age of fourteen I felt like I understood what it was like to feel the way the character felt in that book. I wrote the paper from my heart, and the next day I was placed in a higher-level English class. In that moment, I felt confident for the first time in my life. This moment and this one act of belief from someone else enabled me to write this book, it made me an author and helped me become a thought leader.

Choosing Gratitude

The first step to confidence is to have gratitude for your past and for the person you were. While your past in no way defines your future, it absolutely has an impact on who you are and there is no shame in that. I have yet to meet a truly successful person that has had a perfect past with no failure and nothing to overcome. The most successful and confident people I have ever met generally have had the most struggle in their lives. The difference between someone that is confident or successful and someone who is not has little to do with their past struggles and much to do with the level of gratitude they have.

Just as a blacksmith forging a sword through fire, we are also molded and shaped through hardship, adversity, pressures, and struggles. Diamonds are created through a dance of pressure and heat and like our own journeys, they emerge as radiant beacons of resilience and beauty, reminding us that even amidst life's pressures, we have the power to shine and transform into something truly extraordinary. Even the muscles in our bodies are shaped through resistance and tension and with enough action and time become beautifully formed works of art. Pressure is a catalyst for growth, pushing us to shed our old limitations and embrace a larger, more expansive form. In the face of adversity, we are reminded that it is through embracing and navigating the pressures of life that we, too, can grow, expand, and unlock the vast potential that resides within us.

Our character is developed by these events that often feel like fire, resistance, and pressure. Without these hardships, we cannot properly deliver the service we are meant to render, and we cannot live to our fullest purpose. These events while difficult are all leading us to become the people we are meant to be. If we go through our entire lives without difficulty, you will find that you will not be forged and developed the way you need to be to accomplish your greater purpose and calling in life.

For me to heal, I needed gratitude in my life and giving more helped me begin to feel grateful, even when I felt hopeless. I realized that all those events were a preparation to help me become the person I was always meant to be. I needed to give more to others so that they would have similar revelations in their lives and go on to accomplish their unique purposes. It was also important for me to lead by example and show my daughter the power that gratitude can have on her life, and it worked to uplift, motivate, and inspire both of us to keep going.

It has been scientifically proven that gratitude can rewire our brains and strengthen neural pathways. "Through the power of gratitude, you can wire your brain to be optimistic and compassionate, making you feel good. The more you look, the more you can find to be grateful for. This positivity can extend to those around you, creating a virtuous cycle" ("Neuroscience Reveals: Gratitude", 2020). I want to stress the fact that this is not pseudoscience but factual science with practical application. Gratitude can induce the brain to produce serotonin and dopamine, removing feelings of depression, anxiety, worry, fear, or doubt, and making us feel happier, more relaxed, and less anxious in the short term ("Can Gratitude Improve Quality of Life?", 2022).

Gratitude can also have a more long-lasting effect on

the brain, rewiring it to become more positive and resilient. Rewiring allows our brains to create new neuropathways which in turn help us to be able to form new belief systems and patterns. This is an essential step at building confidence because it carves out the possibility for transformation.

One way that gratitude rewires the brain is by changing the neural pathways that regulate emotions. Studies have shown that when we practice gratitude regularly, we can increase the activity in the prefrontal cortex, which is the part of the brain responsible for regulating emotions and decision-making (Lechner T, 2022). This can help us to become more resilient to stress and better able to cope with challenging situations.

Gratitude can also help to reduce the activity in the amygdala, which is the part of the brain responsible for the fear response (Lechner T, 2022). When we experience fear or live in abusive situations, the amygdala can become overactive, leading to feelings of anxiety and stress. But when we practice gratitude, we can calm the amygdala, reducing our stress levels and helping us to feel more relaxed and at ease, more aware of the present moment and the things that we must be thankful for. This can help us to become more mindful in other areas of our lives, leading to greater levels of happiness and wellbeing, and to healthier relationships with others. When we express gratitude towards others, it can help to strengthen our social bonds and build a sense of community. By practicing gratitude regularly, we can make a positive impact on our own lives and the lives of those around us.

Many practitioners of gratitude claim that it can change your life but how can you have gratitude when you are depressed, anxious, have experienced a painful past, or are currently experiencing trauma? The simple answer is that gratitude is a daily choice and habit and, in every scenario, regardless of the circumstance, for you to heal, you need to choose gratitude. It begins with the understanding that there is always something to be grateful for in your life. It is easy for anyone to get bogged down by their limitations, circumstances, traumas, or limiting beliefs. When you suffer from depression you likely struggle with ruminating thoughts of your past and chances are if you struggle with anxiety your continually thinking of the future and worrying. However, in any situation and regardless of the condition we face, there is always something to be grateful for. When you learn to choose gratitude, you can begin to develop a present mindset. When you are grateful, you appreciate the things and people around you, but you also can have appreciation for how far you have come in life. Through gratitude, you will begin to see your past as a place of evolution instead of intense struggle and you begin to grow as a result. This is why gratitude is the first step to developing confidence. For you to become the confident person you were meant to be, you first need to do the work of rewiring your brain so that you can begin to form new belief systems, patterns, and habits. This lays the foundation for later steps in the process to gaining confidence.

When we can forgive past events or people who have wronged us, we begin the journey of moving forward from our past and into our present and it releases the chains that once bound us. Soon, new beliefs can be formed, and we no longer feel as limited or powerless as we once did. It took me several months to be able to feel gratitude for my past. For so long I was trapped in a victim mindset. I could not understand why I did not have the things that other people seemed to have. I didn't understand why I had a father that was an alcoholic and abusive towards me and I envied other people who came from better circumstances. I thought for many years that because of my past I was a victim, and, in many ways, this victim mentality kept me small and didn't allow me to grow and progress in life. I was so concentrated on what I didn't have that I failed to appreciate the things I did have. For me, the first step towards achieving gratitude for the past was to forgive. I had to forgive my father and my past to progress and move on with my life.

Escaping My Father

The first two times my mother left my father were both during the winter, the first time was the winter of 1993, the second time in 1996. These dates are very easy for me to recall because they all impacted me in different ways. The first time my mother left my father, I was in elementary school. Obviously, my father knew where I went to school, so even though we were not living with him, it was easy for him to find me. At the time, my mother was suffering from a severe nervous breakdown and was on medication, so she was not present-minded. One day as school was dismissed, I got to the front lobby and there my father stood waiting to pick me up. My father had never picked me up from school before. Something didn't feel right but I didn't know what to do so I went with him. Since he was my biological father, the school released me into his custody even though my parents were separated at the time.

My older sister's husband was supposed to pick me up from school but on this day he arrived late. Normally this would have been fine but on this day, I had been kidnapped by my father, it was a perfect storm of unfortunate events. My father and I made it home and I was supposed to pack a bag. I don't remember all the details due to the trauma of the event, but my brother-in-law found us and saved me that day as I was packing my bag. If things would have gone a different way, I may not be here today to write this book. My father's intention was to kidnap me that day so that he could have vengeance on my mother for leaving him, I'm certain of this. Thankfully, I was saved that day and for that

I am grateful.

The second time my mother left my father was during a blizzard. There were snowdrifts six feet high. The day before we left, my mother asked me to pack a bag with clothes, that we would be going to be staying at granddad's house for a few days. I knew exactly what she meant. I wanted out of there and couldn't wait to leave. I have fond memories of warmth, love, and affection during those few days away from my father. My step-grandmother made a lovely tea party for us and homemade butter yellow cupcakes. I can still taste the cupcakes and tea to this day when I think back on that memory. She was a very kind lady and even though we were not biologically related, she treated me as if I were her grandchild. She was the only grandmother I ever had known, and I really loved her.

All the feelings of warmth came crashing down abruptly when my father showed up to my grandfather's home demanding we come back. My grandfather was an old man at the time, but he was a WWII veteran with nerves of steel and a strong distaste for my father. My mother and grandmother rushed me and my older brothers into a bedroom as the two men began to argue, and I could hear my grandfather ask him repeatedly to leave. Then we heard a shotgun being cocked and fired.

It was my grandfather. He had fired a warning shot above my father's head. I will never forget that sound. We were only feet away in another room and I was shaking with terror and crying inconsolably.

My mother broke up the fight and agreed to go back to my father that night. During this incident I was huddled in a corner with my grandmother and older brother, crying and shaking. I didn't want to leave, and I was absolutely terrified of my father. I had felt safe for the first time in my life at my grandfather's house and loved the feeling. The last thing I wanted to do was to go back to the home where I was mistreated and unloved to the man who just days before tried to kidnap me. However, we did just that — in the middle of the night, in the middle of a snowstorm. I cried the entire time and could not understand why this was happening, I thought we had made our grand escape and we were free from him at last. No matter what I said or how much I pleaded it made no difference, and at that moment, I felt as if my voice was gone forever. My opinion and needs seemed to be irrelevant, and no one appeared to care about what was good for me or what I wanted. From that moment on, I struggled deeply with feelings of inadequacy, lack of confidence, depression, and thoughts of suicide that I carried with me into my adult life.

When my mother finally left my father, she told me a few days prior and asked me to keep a secret. I had a calendar in my room, and I drew a heart on the day we were going to leave. I packed my suitcase and put it out of sight under my bed so no one could see it. I put in as much as I could in that suitcase and was prepared to leave everything else behind.

She left him, took me and my two older brothers, and we moved into an apartment a few towns over. Our apartment was not in the best area but to me it was everything. For the first time in my life, I was living somewhere clean that didn't have junk everywhere and while it wasn't the greatest place, it was our place, and I loved it.

However, the excitement started to fade as the court favored partial custody. Since no prior abuse or my kidnapping were not reported to police, there was nothing to prove him to be unsuitable for joint custody. At this time, my older brothers were no longer minors, so I was the only sibling that it impacted. I had thought I was free, that I had finally escaped that house and my father, but I quickly became a pawn and a means for my parents to fight and have arguments. I was forced to visit my father every other weekend, alone. Each time I went, I was so afraid that I slept with a baton next to my bedside just in case I needed to defend myself. It was the only thing I had. Every night before I went to sleep, I prayed to God to get me out of there. During the day, I felt like I had to put a mask and pretend that I wanted to be there just so I wouldn't anger him. This constant need to fake my emotions and feelings took a toll on me and led to me shrinking even more. Not only did I not have a voice, but I also had to pretend to be someone else to survive. I began to feel like a prisoner and couldn't see a way out.

I was in my early teens when these events took place and this experience led to deep feelings of inadequacy and self-loathing which eventually surfaced in the form of body dysmorphia. I believed that I was undesirable, unworthy, and unattractive. I hated my body, I hated the way I looked, and I didn't want to be seen or heard out of fear or judgment or ridicule. The experience of abuse, whether it is physical, emotional, or otherwise can significantly shape a person's self-perception and contribute to the development of body dysmorphia and feelings of inadequacy and when you live in fear and witness abuse, it can make you believe that you are not deserving of more.

The summer before I started high school, my younger cousin spent the night with me at my father's house during visitation. My mother came to pick us up and take us home but before we could leave, my parents began to argue. My father was furious at my mother for leaving and I vividly remember seeing him try to pull my mother out of her car as she held onto the steering wheel. The keys were in the ignition, and he would not let her leave. He broke the key off and half of it remained in the ignition while he held the other half of the key in his hand. My mother shouted "RUN" to my cousin and I who were just feet away in a voice of pure terror that still echoes in my mind to this day.

The fear in her voice was palpable, and I thought that would be the last time I would see her alive. I remember screaming "please stop, please stop" as loud as I possibly could and told my mother that I was not leaving without her. My father made his way inside the home, and I assumed it was to retrieve a gun, but I wasn't sure he would stop there. I began to imagine him killing all of us. A few moments later, after my father began walking towards the house, my mother managed to get out of the vehicle, and we all began to run away from that house as fast as we could. My mother, my cousin and I began to race down our long dirt driveway and made our way towards the road. We were all in obvious distress, crying, shaking, holding each other's hands. Thankfully, someone we knew drove past where we were walking and stopped to see if we were okay. We piled in his truck and that was the last time I ever went back to that house and saw my father.

Soon after, my mother's attorney relayed this incident to the judge, and they deemed my father unfit for joint custody and never made me go back. My mother was able to obtain a restraining order against him, and while it took me a long time to feel safe again, this was a good first step in that direction. However, I continued to look over my shoulder, I was afraid he would come to my school again and kidnap me like he did those years prior while I was in elementary school, and the fear of him finding out where we lived was terrifying. I routinely had dreams of him coming to our apartment with a shot gun and killing us as we slept. I shared a room with my mother in our apartment, and I was convinced that he would barge in the door and shoot at both of our beds as we slept, not caring which one he killed first. When you grow up with this level of fear and insecurity it changes everything about how you view the world.

Forgiveness: A Cure for the Victim Mindset

Getting out of a victim mindset is a process that requires time, effort, and patience. It is important to understand that this mindset can be deeply ingrained, and it may take some work to shift your perspective. But you can begin with these strategies:

- **Acknowledge your feelings.** Recognize that you have been feeling like a victim and allow yourself to feel your emotions fully without judgment. This means being honest with yourself about how you feel and acknowledging any negative thoughts that you may have. By doing this, you can begin to identify the patterns and beliefs that have contributed to your victim mindset.

- **Take responsibility** for your life and the circumstances you find yourself in. This does not mean blaming yourself for what has happened to you, but rather recognizing that you have the power to change your situation. When you take responsibility, you are taking ownership of your life and your actions. You are no longer a passive victim of your circumstances, but an active participant in your life.

- **Reframe your perspective.** Shift your focus from what you don't have or what you can't do, to what you can do and what you do have. Instead of seeing problems as insurmountable obstacles, view them as challenges to overcome as well as opportunities for growth and learning. This can help you approach them with a more positive and proactive mindset. You can begin to see things in a more positive light and find new solutions to old problems.

- **Practice gratitude.** We have already seen how powerful it can be when you make a conscious effort to focus on the positive aspects of your life and express gratitude for them. This can help shift your mindset from one of victimhood to one of abundance. When you focus on what you do have, you are more likely to attract positive experiences into your life and be present-minded.

- **Seek support.** Surround yourself with positive and supportive people who will encourage and motivate you to make positive changes in your life. Consider seeking the help of a therapist, mentor, coach, or counselor if you need additional support. Having a support system can help you stay accountable and motivated on your journey towards a more empowered mindset.

Ultimately, we cannot leave the victim mindset behind until we learn to forgive. Forgiveness can be quite challenging, especially if someone has abused you or wronged you in your life. I am not trying to make the act of forgiveness seem trivial, it takes a great deal of mental fortitude and courage to forgive someone what has hurt you. However, it is one of the best decisions you can make because the longer you hold onto resentment of a person or event that has happened to you, the longer you stay a victim of them. I realized as an adult that the more I thought about my father and focused on what I didn't have, the less I was concentrating on what I wanted out of life and where I wanted to go. I was unintentionally living in the past by concentrating on it and not forgiving it. The reason I wasn't progressing had less to do about my circumstances and more to do with my mindset. I knew that I no longer wanted to be a mental prisoner of my past and it was time for me to forgive and move forward. While I am not condoning my father's behavior, through my forgiveness I am choosing to move on and no longer be his victim.

As you progress in your journey in life there will be hardships, events, failures, and circumstances that can impact you or weigh you down if you let them. Remember, these are lessons not life sentences, unless you allow them to be. Forgive and move past those circumstances by practicing gratitude for these lessons because they have all worked to shape your story and who you are today. Without forgiveness you cannot truly have gratitude and if you don't practice gratitude, you will never reach your fullest potential. Consistent acts of devout gratitude are essential for developing high levels of confidence because truly confident people do not hold on to their past, they are not victims of circumstances, and they see obstacles as learning opportunities that propel them into advancement.

The View from 10,000 Feet

If forgiveness or gratitude for your past is a difficult concept for you to understand or achieve, take into consideration an alternate perspective to help you achieve the desired result. Since you lived your past, you have emotional ties to it, so it can be challenging to detach. However, taking a bird's eye view of your past can help.

Consider a hawk in the sky in search of prey on the ground. The hawk's view grants it the ability to see everything happening on the ground below. It can spot a mouse from across a field and sees everything in between. The hawk has a completely different perspective of everything happening on the ground compared to the mouse in the field. The mouse sees what is directly in front of him and is caught up in everything happening to him on the ground, the mouse can't see his way out of his own situation due to his limited perspective. However, the hawk can see the mouse and anticipate the next move it will make. The perspective of the hawk allows for calm and calculated movements. Anytime you get caught up in not being able to have gratitude for past events due to emotion or trauma consider how the situation looks like from above —ask yourself what positive things those experiences brought you in the long term.

Some examples of questions you can ask yourself are:

- How did your difficult situation help you become the person you are today?
- How did those trials equip you to handle your purpose?
- How did your trauma make it possible for you to relate to someone else and help them?
- How did your failure propel you to achieve

something greater?

- How did your heartbreak make you well-suited to counsel others based on your experience?

Hardships when viewed from the ground level seem nearly insurmountable. To have gratitude for them, a higher view must be taken so that you have the appreciation for them and the lessons they taught you as a result. Another way to get a bird's eye view of the trauma in your past is to try to better understand the person who hurt you – to understand why they did what they did or how they became the person they were. My father had a hard upbringing. He lived in poverty his entire life and was surrounded by alcoholism. His mother's family were poor immigrants from Hungary and his father's family were coal miners from West Virginia. Both his mother and father lived through the great depression and in poverty their entire lives. I recall as a little girl watching my grandmother wash and reuse paper towels, straws, and even aluminum foil. She grew up so incredibly poor and kept the mindset and habits of poverty, even into adulthood. My father grew up with nothing and didn't have much hope for advancement in his life. He tuned to alcohol, drugs, and never followed normal societal standards. To be clear, this story does not absolve my father of the way he abused me, my mother, or my siblings, but it does shed light on the explanation for his behavior and tendencies as an adult. Understanding where he came from that led him to be so troubled helped me get the 10,000-foot view I needed to forgive him and move on with my life.

Forgiveness does not mean that you must tolerate abuse or allow the person who abused you back into your life. It's important to set boundaries to protect yourself and to make sure that you feel safe. Remember, forgiveness is a deeply personal journey and process that takes time. It's important to be patient and kind to yourself as you work through the process of forgiveness.

I never saw my father after the age of fourteen and at the point I am writing this book, I have lived more years without him than I had with him. Since the last time I saw my father, I have graduated high school, college (more than once), gotten married and had a family. All of which my father failed to experience. To this day he has no idea my daughter exists, and I can't help but think of all the things he has missed out on that a normal grandfather would enjoy. The fact that he will go the rest of his life without seeing us is truly saddening. As I write this book my father in in his late seventies, alone, with no family, and with no friends. He will likely die alone in the home I grew up in which at this point has to be dilapidated and unlivable by most people's standards. I used to be terrified of him, I used to hide from him, now I can only imagine how the years have taken a toll on him, and the man who I was once terrified of, I now pity. While the emotional scars took many years to heal, they are nothing compared to the loneliness he must be facing at this point in his life.

If you have faced abuse, trauma, or have lived in poverty and have not resolved it, I encourage anyone reading this to seek help and guidance. Overcoming the trauma of an abusive childhood can be a challenging and complex process, but it is possible with the right support and resources. Consider reaching out to a mental health professional or therapist who can provide specialized support and guidance in dealing with the aftermath of abuse. A therapist can help you process your emotions, develop coping mechanisms, and work through any traumatic memories or experiences. Surround yourself with positive, supportive people who believe in you and encourage your growth. This can include friends, family members, and support groups. It's important to have people you can rely on to provide emotional support and validation. Taking care of your physical and emotional needs is crucial to the healing process, too. Engage in activities that make you feel good, such as exercise, meditation, or hobbies. Make sure you're getting enough sleep, eating a balanced diet, and taking time for yourself. Say no to things that don't serve you and set limits with people who may trigger negative emotions or behaviors. This may include limiting your interactions with friends and family members who don't represent the person you are evolving into. You may find as you journey into your most confident self that your circle becomes smaller. The people who were once a part of your life may not suite your new goals and trajectory. This is perfectly normal and a part of the growth process.

Remember that healing from an abusive childhood is a

unique and personal journey but like anything else, it is a choice. Be patient with yourself, and trust that with time and support, you can overcome the trauma and live a fulfilling, joyful, and confident life. When we forgive, it releases us from mental imprisonment so while this process can be challenging, it is incredibly rewarding.

Practice these positive affirmations to develop gratitude for your past. Say them as many times as it takes for you to heal and appreciate your past experiences for making you who you are today:

1. I am grateful for my past experiences because they shaped me into the person I am today.
2. My past has provided me with valuable lessons and wisdom that I can use to create a brighter future with opportunity.
3. I am thankful for the challenges I have faced in the past because they have taught me resilience and strength.
4. Every experience from my past has led me to where I am now, and for that, I am grateful.
5. I choose to focus on the positive memories and experiences from my past, and I am grateful for each one.

6. I am thankful for the opportunities that came my way in the past, and I trust that more opportunities will present themselves in the future.
7. My past has helped me grow and evolve as a person, and I am grateful for that growth.
8. I am thankful for the people who have been a part of my past, and the memories we have shared together.
9. Every moment from my past has contributed to the person I am today, and for that, I am grateful.
10. I am grateful for the blessings that have come my way in the past, and I trust that more blessings will come.

Takeaways from this Chapter:

- *Acknowledge Your Growth:* By expressing gratitude for your past, you can recognize how far you've come. Embrace the experiences, both positive and challenging, that have shaped you into the person you are today. Celebrate your growth and progress.
- *Find Wisdom in Mistakes, Failures & Trauma:* Instead of dwelling on regrets, view your past mistakes as opportunities for learning and growth. Gratitude allows

you to extract valuable lessons from these experiences and avoid repeating the same errors in the future.

- *Release Resentment:* Gratitude helps you let go of past grievances and resentments. Holding onto negative emotions from the past can be draining and prevent you from fully enjoying the present. Embrace forgiveness and choose to focus on the positive aspects of your journey.
- *Cultivate a Positive Mindset:* When you are grateful for your past, you shift your focus from what went wrong to what went right. This change in mindset can have a profound impact on your overall attitude and outlook on life.
- *Appreciate the Present Moment:* Gratitude for your past experiences can bring you into the present moment. When you are grateful for where you've been, you become more mindful of your current circumstances and can find joy in the little things.
- *Recognize Strengths and Resilience:* Your past likely holds moments of triumph over challenges and difficulties. Expressing gratitude for these instances helps you acknowledge your strengths and resilience, boost-

ing your self-confidence.

- *Foster Self-Compassion:* Gratitude allows you to be kinder to yourself. Instead of being overly critical of past decisions, show yourself compassion and understanding. Remember that you did the best you could with the knowledge and resources available at the time.
- *Embrace Change:* Life is a series of changes and transitions. Gratitude helps you accept and embrace these changes, understanding that each phase of life contributes to your growth and development.
- *Nurture Optimism:* Gratitude fuels optimism for the future. When you appreciate the positive aspects of your past, you cultivate hope and belief in better things to come.

Lessons Learned from Having Gratitude for Your Past:
- *The Power of Perspective:* Viewing your past through a lens of gratitude provides a new perspective on your life story. You begin to see challenges as opportunities for growth and setbacks as stepping stones toward success.

- *A Foundation for Resilience:* Gratitude strengthens your resilience by reminding you of your ability to overcome past obstacles. You gain confidence in your capacity to handle future challenges with grace and determination.
- *Living with Intention:* Being grateful for your past encourages you to live with intention in the present. You become more mindful of your choices and actions, understanding their potential impact on your future self.
- *Creating Positive Ripples:* Expressing gratitude for your past can inspire others to do the same. Your gratitude becomes infectious and can create a ripple effect of positivity in your relationships and within communities.
- *A Source of Empowerment:* Gratitude empowers you to take ownership of your life. You realize that you have the power to shape your narrative and can use your past experiences as a catalyst for personal growth and fulfillment.

Embrace the gift of gratitude for your past, and you'll find that it becomes a powerful tool for living a fulfilling and meaningful life. When you acknowledge the value of your past experiences, you open the door to a future filled with possibilities and gratitude for every step along the way.

Your Turn:

1.) Write a few lessons or experiences from your past that helped shape you into the person you are today:

2.) How did your past equip you with resilience?

3.) What are 10 experiences or lessons from your past that you are grateful for?

Chapter 2: Gratitude for the Person You Are

My unresolved traumas from childhood continued to impact me into my adult life in many ways. As I went into the workforce, I found myself drifting from company to company and job to job. I went from one toxic workplace to another. Corporate jobs were the furthest thing from my childhood that I could find, and I thought if I had a job in corporate my life would finally be the way I wanted it to be. However, this was far from the case. During my career I had several male managers belittle me, yell at me, tell me my work was flawed, and not support me. I thought I wanted to go into the corporate world and become successful but all the while I was chasing someone else's version of what success was.

None of my corporate colleagues knew of my past and within large organizations I felt like I could blend in. I tried desperately to fit in, but I felt as if I was wearing a mask once again, just as I did when I was a little girl. I went above and beyond to please my employer and to show that I was valuable, worthy, and smart. I would outwork everyone in the attempt to receive praise and validation. I had difficulty saying no and always took on more work than I could handle. I often worked through lunch, was the first to come in and the last to leave. I was always trying to prove myself and my worth and do more than anyone. I was becoming unhealthy physically and mentally and every time I said "yes" to something else, my sense of confidence diminished even further.

Any validation I received from my employers was always short-lived and did not carry the weight that I was looking for to make myself feel whole and worthy. No matter how fantastic my performance, I was always left feeling like they wanted and expected more, once again in my life I wasn't enough. Regardless of how I performed that day, the next day more was expected. It felt like I was chasing someone else's dream, living someone else's life, and pretending to be someone I was not. No one knew the real me, no one knew what I had been through or was going through, and inside,

I started to feel even more empty. When you go through your entire life wearing a mask and not letting people in, it deepens your limiting beliefs, leads to negative self-talk, self-doubt, and imposter syndrome. No matter how smart, beautiful, or talented you are, you never feel whole when you are living an inauthentic life, it makes it impossible to forge meaningful relationships with others and ultimately leads to profound sadness and loneliness.

I believe, on a subconscious level, I was so reliant on the validation from others because as a child I received no validation or praise from my father. During my career as I went from one toxic leader and company to another, I continually sought approval and attention from my managers. All I wanted was for someone to validate me and believe in my abilities. I regularly sought out men for compliments about my appearance to feel validated, which only leads to heart break and deepens feelings of self-doubt and lack of confidence. But looks weren't enough — I also sought to validate my self-worth by amassing credentials. Certification after certification and degree after degree, I continually sought to become more qualified and more educated. I would say to myself things like, "if I just receive one more degree, one more piece of paper, or one more credential I will be respected, people will like me, and I will be where I want to be." I was always chasing the high of "one more." Eventually, validation becomes a drug, and you are always left chasing, but the high is short-lived and never enough to get your fix permanently.

The Trap of External Validation

External validation provides a temporary high that can be addictive. When we receive validation from others, whether it's in the form of praise, compliments, or recognition, it can feel good. This is because validation activates the reward centers in our brain, releasing dopamine, a neurotransmitter associated with pleasure and motivation (Gardner E.L., 2011). However, just like a drug, the effects of external validation are temporary and fleeting. We may feel good in the moment, but over time, we can become dependent on it to feel good about ourselves. This can lead to a cycle of seeking validation from others, rather than developing a strong sense of self-worth and self-validation. This is another reason why gratitude is the first step at building confidence, it enables you to produce dopamine from another source other than external validation. Seeking external validation can also be problematic because it puts us at the mercy of others' opinions and judgments. We may become overly focused on pleasing others and conforming to their expectations, rather than being true to ourselves and our values. This can lead to feelings of anxiety, insecurity, and self-doubt, as we constantly seek the approval of others to feel good about ourselves. External validation can be like a drug because it provides a temporary high that can be addictive. However, just like a drug, it can also be harmful if we become too dependent on it and neglect our own sense of self-worth and self-validation. It's important to strive for a healthy balance between seeking validation from others and developing a strong sense of self-esteem and self-validation.

It is possible to build the confidence necessary to self-validate. You can start by exploring yourself and identifying areas where you are experiencing lack of confidence and areas where you feel that validation from others is necessary.

- When you accomplish something do you feel it necessary to tell others to receive a compliment or affirmation?
- Do you feel discouraged when others fail to compliment you, recognize you or acknowledge you or your work?
- Do you feel that for people to like you, respect you, or do business with you that you need to have more degrees, more certifications, need to look better, speak better, or be more successful?

Chances are most people reading these questions relate on some level and have experienced this in their lives. However, I know from lived experience you will never think that you are enough if you continually believe that you need more of something external to validate yourself. True confidence starts with the acknowledgement that you are enough as you are. Truly confident people are not reliant on a drug like outside validation to keep them motivated, and they do not seek the opinions of others to feel accomplished. True confidence is about being whole as you are and owning **your** power. Every time you seek outside validation to experience confidence and worth you are giving a piece of your power away, and eventually there will be no more pieces left to give. You will be reduced, diminished and powerless. Confidence begins the moment you decide you are whole and enough just as you are, and it continues with daily practice and through gratitude.

You Deserve More

Do you believe in your heart that you deserve more, are made for more, are worth more, or want to be happier? Believing that you deserve more and are worth more can be a powerful motivator in helping you see what you can achieve. When you believe that you are worthy of success, confidence, and happiness, you are more likely to take risks, set higher goals, and work harder to achieve them. Having a strong sense of self-worth can also help you to develop a more positive mindset and outlook on life. You are more likely to approach challenges with a growth mindset, seeing obstacles as opportunities for learning and growth rather than as barriers to success.

Believing in your worth can help you to identify and

pursue opportunities that align with your values and goals. When you know that you deserve more, you are less likely to settle for less than what you want and can achieve. Believing that you deserve more and are worth more can also help you to develop stronger boundaries and self-advocacy skills. When you recognize your own worth, you are more likely to assert yourself in situations where you feel undervalued or mistreated. Overall, believing that you deserve more and are worth more can be a powerful force in helping you to see what you can achieve. It can help you to develop a stronger sense of self, cultivate a positive mindset, pursue your goals with greater determination, and ultimately achieve greater success and fulfillment in your life.

The fact that you picked up this book is proof enough that you know in your heart that you are capable of more. Something within you knows you deserve more, and you invested in yourself by purchasing this book. **THIS IS SPARK**, and a little bit of spark is all you need to become the confident and dynamic person you want to be. Whatever you do, don't let this spark pass you by, act on it immediately and intentionally.

What's Holding You Back?

For those of us that have had a traumatic past, a troubled upbringing, or a family that was unsupportive, negative, or abusive it may seem insurmountable to gain confidence, especially if you feel that someone has taken something away from you. What in your present situation creates feelings of lack of self-worth? Perhaps you are in a workplace that is toxic or have a negative boss who works to diminish your self-worth like mine did. It could also be a romantic relationship, friendships, or family members that lead you to feeling unconfident about yourself. Whatever it is, get clear on how people or situations make you feel and start to identify them. If your workplace, friendships, or relationships are making you feel this way, I promise you, they are not worth being around. No amount of money can replace a sense of diminished self-worth and feelings of inadequacy, and the longer you associate yourself and surround yourself with toxicity, the more you begin to believe what people say about you is factual.

The people you surround yourself with will either work to build you up or tear you down, there is no grey area here. Believe me when I say there is nothing worth the price of your peace of mind, just as there is nothing worth the price of you feeling less confident about yourself. Your life begins the moment you accept this fact. Do not under any circumstance let anyone take away your or diminish your confidence, guard it at all costs and be mindful of how people impact the feelings you have about yourself.

The Toxic Workplace

If you are in a toxic workplace, it can have a significant negative impact on your overall well-being, sense of self-worth, and mental health, producing outcomes like:

- **Stress:** Toxic workplaces are often characterized by an environment of negativity, criticism, and hostility, which can lead to chronic stress that can manifest as physical symptoms such as headaches, digestive issues, and weakened immune systems, as well as mental health issues like anxiety and depression.
- **Burnout:** Burnout is a state of physical, emotional,

and mental exhaustion caused by prolonged exposure to a stressful work environment. In a toxic workplace, the lack of support, high workload, and negative attitudes can contribute to burnout and feelings of being overwhelmed.

- **Negative Self-Image:** Negative feedback, criticism, and bullying can cause you to doubt your abilities and feel insecure in your role. This can lead to a negative self-image and a lack of confidence. Isolation is another detrimental effect of being in a toxic workplace. Toxic workplaces often lack a supportive and collaborative culture, which can contribute to a sense of isolation and disconnection from others. This can further exacerbate mental health issues such as depression and anxiety.
- **Decreased Job Satisfaction and motivation.** When you are constantly exposed to negativity and toxicity, it can be challenging to find meaning and purpose in your work. This can lead to a lack of motivation and decreased productivity.

Despite all these negative outcomes, many women will

feel obligated to stay in a toxic work environment and continue to prove their worth. Smart, qualified, educated, and successful women often struggle to believe in their worth, settling for less than they deserve. A variety of factors contribute — social conditioning, imposter syndrome, fear of failure, lack of confidence, and personal insecurities. Society often reinforces gender stereotypes that undervalue women, and those who were raised to prioritize others' needs may struggle with prioritizing their own. Imposter syndrome can cause smart and successful women to doubt their abilities and feel like they don't belong. Fear of failure can prevent women from taking risks and pursuing their goals, leading them to settle for less than they deserve. Women may also lack confidence in their abilities due to a lack of representation of women in leadership roles or a lack of support and encouragement from others. Personal insecurities can also cause women to undervalue themselves and believe they are not deserving of success.

For many years in my career, I struggled with self-worth, and I lacked confidence to negotiate my salary. Unfortunately, I wasn't alone. Many smart, talented, and hard-working women are afraid to ask for what they deserve, and this further contributes to gender pay inequity. Societal expectations, stereotypes, and backlash against assertive behavior can make women hesitant to negotiate or penalized when they do. Negotiation outcomes can also be influenced by power imbalances and employer practices. When a woman has had past trauma as I did, negotiation in the workplace seems terrifying and as a result, you make substantially less than your peers. This reinforces the belief system that you lack value and are not enough.

Female leadership statistics show that women are underrepresented in top leadership positions across various industries and sectors. Even though research has shown that having more diverse leadership teams can lead to better financial performance and innovation, only around 10% of Fortune 500 CEO positions are currently held by women and in the United States and women only hold approximately 30% of senior management positions (Elting L, 2023). It can feel like an uphill battle to climb to the top in corporate as a woman but if you are lacking in confidence it can seem like climbing a mountain.

For years in my career, I didn't negotiate my salary, benefits, or anything that would help me advance. I accepted my first offer because I didn't feel worthy of more, despite being highly educated and experienced. It is my mission to help women build their confidence so that this doesn't happen to them. I want to show women that no matter what you have been through or are going through, you are worth every penny, don't undervalue yourself. Developing the confidence to negotiate your salary is an important step for women in closing the gender pay gap and building confidence.

When I quit my toxic corporate job I said, "enough is enough" I had an incredibly low self-esteem and sense of self-worth, but there was a spark inside me that lit the fuse and worked to ignite my full potential. While small, it existed within me and empowered me to believe in myself. A stick of dynamite does not need a forest fire to be ignited, it needs a single spark and the destruction it is capable of from that single spark creates a major impact on everything surrounding it. Never underestimate the impact a seemingly small spark can have in your life and what it can do for your confidence. That small spark could very well be enough to change your life forever. The realization dawned upon me that I possessed untapped potential and a burning desire to carve my own path. With newfound courage and self-belief, I took a leap of faith, leaving behind the familiar confines of the corporate world to embark on a journey of self-discovery and entrepreneurship, confident in my ability to create a life aligned with my passions and dreams. For the first time, I dared to believe in myself and found the freedom to pursue my dreams fearlessly.

Validation from Strangers

Before I learned to step into true confidence I struggled deeply with feelings of incompletion. I continually searched for validation. I would look in the mirror and no matter what I looked like on the outside, I felt ugly and undesirable inside. As I began my journey into full-time entrepreneurship after leaving my corporate career, I had to market myself and put myself out there to the world in a way I never imagined before. I went from not posting on social media to posting every day, sometimes multiple times per day. Very quickly I went from being an introvert who was deeply struggling with depression and confidence to someone in the public eye, and attention started pouring in. It was difficult to handle at first and not all the attention I received was positive. Some of the attention I received was wonderful, it led to increases in opportunities, clients, and helped me grow my business. However, some of the attention I received worked to bring my confidence down even further. Women are often the targets of misogynistic comments, threats, and explicit messages on social media platforms. This type of behavior can create a hostile online environment for women, making it difficult for them to express themselves freely and feel confident online. Women are often subjected to cyberbullying, body shaming, and online harassment on social media. Negative comments, hurtful messages, and online trolling can deeply impact self-esteem and confidence. The anonymity of the online world can embolden individuals to engage in hurtful behavior, causing significant emotional distress.

The best thing you can do to show up online confidently is to seek out online communities and connections that uplift and support you. Engage with like-minded individuals who inspire and encourage you and build a network of positive support can boost your confidence and provide a safe space to share and engage authentically. Practice positive self-talk to counteract any negative self-perception or self-doubt that may arise from online interactions. Remind yourself of your strengths, achievements, and the value you bring to the online space. Affirmations and positive self-talk can help boost your confidence and resilience. Recognize when you need a break from social media or online interactions. Regularly prioritize self-care activities that nourish your well-being and help you recharge. Remember that your online presence is just one aspect of your life. Do not rely on external validation from social media to build confidence, if you do, you will get caught up in an endless cycle of attention-seeking behavior. While social media is an essential aspect of building your personal brand and business, it also promotes constant comparison with others, leading to feelings of inadequacy and low self-esteem. The constant pursuit of likes, comments, and followers creates a reliance on external validation for self-worth, diminishing one's belief in their intrinsic value. The pressure to present a perfect image on social media can lead to inauthenticity and a fear of being judged, further undermining confidence. Social media platforms often showcase carefully curated and filtered versions of people's lives, emphasizing their successes, achievements, and glamorous moments.

Occasionally disconnect from social media and digital platforms to recalibrate and focus on your offline life. Use this time to engage in activities that bring you joy, nurture relationships, and pursue personal growth. Taking breaks from the online world can help reduce comparison and restore confidence. Lift others up and celebrate their achievements and successes instead of comparing yourself to them. Engage in positive and constructive interactions with others, fostering a supportive and empowering online community. By championing others, you contribute to a positive online environment while boosting your own confidence.

The Seed of Confidence Is Within You

Acknowledging your present state is a necessary step in the unfolding of the person you are to become. Through acknowledgement and self-awareness, it becomes possible to change old ways of doing things, habits, and make necessary improvements needed in your life. Just as it is necessary to understand and be thankful for our past selves, it is also necessary to forgive our present selves and to show gratitude for our present state, even if we are not yet where we want to be in life. The foundation for growth is forgiveness and by having profound gratitude for what you have in your life. The power of gratitude is that it's an endless resource; no matter what circumstances you have faced or what you have had to overcome in your life, there is always something to be grateful for. Gratitude will change your life, but it is a choice you need to make daily.

    With all things, in all circumstances, find gratitude. Every cell in your body is working to keep you alive right now, your cells are collaborating on a collective scale to keep you thriving. If you are presently in a position in life which is unfavorable to you, finding gratitude for the simple fact that you are alive is enough reason to be appreciative. The longer and more often you concentrate on things you don't want or have in life, the less you will receive in proportion. It is my firm belief that when we find gratitude and show appreciation, we receive more positivity and abundance in return. When you show gratitude for how far you have come in life and acknowledge lessons learned you will begin to realize that you hold the power to have the future you want. To achieve your desired future outcome, start by appreciating how far you have come in your journey. It is easy to get caught up in busy daily activity, but it is important to show thankful acknowledgement. Remind yourself daily what you have done and what you can do and say it with power and conviction until you believe it to be so.

Think of confidence as a seed that is lying dormant awaiting an opportunity to sprout. For confidence to sprout it needs to be nurtured, cultivated, supported, and given proper care. It also takes time for that seed to become a plant full of life and potential, so try not get discouraged if it takes some time to develop but have faith that it is blossoming and evolving within you.

Seeds naturally work on their purpose if their needs are supported. An apple seed for example does not require proof of its reason for being here or question its ability to become a tree, it simply sprouts and goes into action to become what it was designed for. Just like a seed needs the right conditions to grow and thrive, confidence requires the right mindset and environment to develop. It needs nourishment in the form of positive self-talk, encouragement, and support. By surrounding yourself with positivity, you can create an environment that is conducive to grow and develop confidence.

You can cultivate your confidence by focusing on your strengths, setting achievable goals, and taking small steps towards your goals. Just as a seed can grow into a fully mature plant that bears fruit, confidence can also lead to positive outcomes in your life. By believing in yourself and your abilities, you can achieve your goals and live a fulfilling life. By nurturing your confidence like a seed, you can create the right conditions for growth and development, leading to a more positive and fulfilling life. The power of metamorphose exists within us all and if there is a seed of confidence and a spark within you that wants more out of life than what you are currently experiencing, you have the capacity to become the most confident version of yourself with enough time and persistence. This spark saved my life in more ways than one, but it is a lesson I needed to keep relearning until it was firmly solidified in my mind and heart.

Practice these positive affirmations to develop gratitude for your present. Say them as many times as it takes for you to appreciate your present reality, how far you have come in life, and what you have:

1. I am grateful for this moment, and I choose to make the most of it.
2. I appreciate the beauty and wonder of the world around me, and I am thankful for the small things in life.
3. I am thankful for my health and well-being, and I take care of my body, mind, and spirit.
4. I am surrounded by love and positivity, and I am grateful for the people who support and care for me.
5. I am thankful for the opportunities and possibilities that are available to me in the present moment.
6. I am grateful for the talents and skills that I possess, and I am excited to use them to create a better life.
7. I am thankful for the challenges that I face in the

present moment, as they help me grow and learn.

8. I am grateful for my job/career, and I am thankful for the income and stability it provides me.

9. I appreciate the relationships in my life, and I am grateful for the connections and memories we share.

10. I am thankful for my personal growth and evolution, and I am excited to see where my journey takes me in the future.

Takeaways from this Chapter:

- *Practice Mindfulness:* Cultivate gratitude for your present self by practicing mindfulness. Be fully present in the moment, embracing the experiences, emotions, and sensations that arise without judgment.

- *Celebrate Achievements, Big & Small:* Acknowledge and celebrate your accomplishments, no matter how significant or minor they may seem. Gratitude for your present self involves recognizing your efforts and progress, boosting self-esteem and motivation.

- *Accept Imperfections & Embrace Strengths:* Embrace gratitude for your imperfections and vulnerabilities.

Remember that being human means being flawed, and these imperfections contribute to your uniqueness and growth. However, we each have unique strengths and gifts so embrace what you are naturally gifted at.

- *Appreciate Self-Care:* Value the importance of self-care and self-compassion. Gratitude for your present self means taking care of your physical, emotional, and mental well-being, allowing you to thrive and be more present for others.
- *Focus on Positivity*: Redirect your attention to the positive aspects of your life. Gratitude can shift your perspective, enabling you to see the abundance and blessings around you, even during challenging times.
- *Practice Gratitude Journaling:* Keep a gratitude journal to document the things you are grateful for each day. This practice helps you become more aware of the positive elements in your life and fosters a sense of appreciation for your present self.
- *Be Kind to Yourself:* Treat yourself with kindness and compassion. Gratitude for your present self involves

avoiding self-criticism and negative self-talk, promoting a healthier and more loving relationship with yourself.

- *Find Joy in Everyday Moments:* Take pleasure in the simple joys of life. Gratitude encourages you to notice and savor the little moments that bring happiness and contentment to your day.
- *Express Gratitude to Others:* Extend your gratitude to the people in your life who support and care for you. Showing appreciation strengthens your relationships and fosters a sense of interconnectedness.

Lessons Learned from Having Gratitude for Your Present Self:

- *Enhanced Well-Being:* Gratitude for your present self is linked to improved overall well-being. It boosts happiness, reduces stress, and promotes a positive outlook on life.
- *Building Resilience:* By appreciating your current strengths and resources, you become better equipped to face life's challenges. Gratitude nurtures resilience

and the ability to bounce back from adversity.

- *Fostering Self-Growth:* Gratitude encourages personal growth and self-improvement. When you appreciate your present self, you are more motivated to continue learning, evolving, and pursuing your goals.
- *Deepening Relationships:* A genuine sense of gratitude radiates to those around you, deepening your connections with others. Your appreciation for your present self inspires others to do the same, creating a positive and supportive environment.
- *Living in Abundance:* Gratitude shifts your focus from what is lacking to what you have in abundance. It opens your eyes to the richness of your life, allowing you to be content with what you already possess.
- *Inspiring Generosity:* Gratitude fuels a desire to give back and help others. When you are thankful for your present self, you are more likely to extend kindness and support to those in need.
- *A Foundation for Future Success:* Gratitude for your present self-lays the groundwork for future achievements. When you value and appreciate your current

efforts, you cultivate the motivation to pursue new opportunities and endeavors.

Embrace gratitude for your present self as a transformative practice that nurtures self-love, contentment, and growth. Remember that you are a unique and valuable individual deserving of appreciation and kindness. Gratitude opens the door to a fulfilling and meaningful life, where you can embrace the present moment with joy and optimism.

Your Turn:

1.) What people or things need to be removed from your present life to surround yourself with more positivity and less negativity?

2.) What steps are you willing to take to remove negativity or toxicity from your life?

3.) What are 10 things in your present life that you are grateful for:

Chapter 3: Gratitude for the Person You Are Becoming

During therapy I went on a journey of self-discovery to heal past wounds and face past trauma once and for all. I began to uncover sufferings from childhood that were suppressed and started to understand why and how they were impacting present behaviors. Realizing these deep truths gave me powerful insight into blockages that were preventing me from moving forward with my life, achieving my goals, and stepping into my power. However, the most powerful truth I learned through therapy was how much I was reliant on attention from external validation to feel confident and whole within myself.

Through therapy I learned to finally forgive my father, forgive my past, and forgive myself for my mistakes. During a session with my therapist, he asked me to imagine myself as a little girl. I thought about what I would say to her and what she needed to hear. What could I tell her to finally become confident and successful? In my visual, I pictured myself hugging that little girl. I told her that she was smart, brave, beautiful, and that one day she would grow up to become confident and accomplish her wildest dreams. I assured her that she was worthy and that she would overcome her obstacles and adversity to go onto live a wonderful and happy life. This seemingly simple exercise allowed me to finally leave the past where it belongs and move on. It also reminded me how far I have come in my life, and it filled my heart with intense gratitude. The little girl I saw in my visual would grow up to own her power and she didn't need outside validation to be whole, that she was whole as she was. From that moment on, I began to finally start to feel confident and stay that way.

My last session with the therapist was intensely emotional, and I couldn't help but cry. I felt as if my soul was being revealed. My therapist asked me to close my eyes, and I took several deep and calming breaths. I focused on my breathing and did my best to clear my mind. My therapist asked me to visualize the most confident and successful version of myself and say the first things that came to my mind. I instantly pictured a woman that looked amazing, wearing heels, a beautiful dress, who walked with poise and grace. Her smile lit up every room she was in, her shoulders were pulled back, and she was stunning to look at. I pictured her walking to her car and getting in and letting her convertible top down. This woman did not rely on compliments, accolades, or attention from men or anyone to feel confident, she was naturally this way and it shined through. No one questioned her background, education, or where she came from, they automatically had respect for her and listened to her every word because she exuded confidence.

The most confident version of yourself is comfortable in their own skin and has a positive self-image. They are self-assured and assertive, and they have a clear understanding of their strengths and weaknesses. They are not afraid to take risks, speak their mind, or pursue their goals, even in the face of obstacles or setbacks. They are resilient and adaptable, and they view challenges as opportunities for growth and learning. They are also empathetic and compassionate towards others, and they inspire confidence and trust in those around them. The most confident version of yourself radiates a sense of self-belief, purpose, and inner strength, which will allow you to navigate life's ups and downs with grace and resilience.

Visualizing your most confident self is a powerful technique that can help you develop self-confidence and overcome feelings of self-doubt. Imagine yourself as your ideal self, with all the qualities and traits that you admire. Pay attention to your body language and visualize yourself standing tall, speaking clearly, and projecting confidence in everything you do. Focus on a specific situation where you would like to feel more confident and imagine yourself in that situation, handling any challenges or obstacles with ease and grace. Use positive affirmations to reinforce your beliefs and repeat them often. Visualization is a skill that can be developed with regular practice, so set aside a few minutes each day to practice. Remember, visualization is just one tool for building self-confidence, so act towards your goals and seek support from others when needed. With practice and determination, you can become the confident and self-assured person you want to be. The mental visuals that we tell ourselves help steer us in the right direction. If you can visualize it, you can become it.

Once I had a visual of what real confidence looked like and felt like, there was no going back. My entire life I had never given much thought about how reliant I was on the validation of others to make myself feel confident. I had never thought how addicted I was to attention and how empty I felt immediately afterwards. Therapy helped me recover from my addictive and destructive cycle of external validation. Finally, it was time to heal the wounds of my past once and for all and become the person I was meant to be. It was time to step into real unfiltered and unabashed confidence.

To become the most effective mentor and leader for my team, my clients, my business, my family, and myself I knew I needed to make some serious changes. The woman I saw in my vision was a strong and decisive individual who is not afraid to take risks or make difficult decisions. Her confidence is reflected in her posture, tone of voice, and the way she carries herself. She has a clear vision for her organization and is not afraid to communicate it to her team.

She is an excellent communicator, able to articulate her ideas clearly and concisely. She is also a great listener, taking the time to hear out the perspectives of others and incorporating their feedback into her decision-making process. This leader is knowledgeable and well-informed about the industry and the issues that affect her organization. She is constantly seeking to expand her knowledge and stay up to date on the latest trends and developments. She is also able to inspire and motivate her team, creating a positive and supportive work environment. Overall, she is respected and admired by her team, colleagues, and peers. She is a role model for other women in leadership positions, demonstrating that with hard work, dedication, and self-belief, anyone can achieve great success. Most importantly, she is a confident and devoted wife and mother who demonstrates strength, resilience, and grace with every action. Now that I was armed with the vision of who I wanted to become it was time to for me to step out of my comfort zone and start living aligned with this vision.

The Surprising Power of Manifesting

Having gratitude for the person you are becoming may seem like a strange concept but many experts in manifesting agree that when you display gratitude for things and have appreciation for them before you have yet to receive them you are in many ways signaling to the universe that you have already achieved it. This signaling sets off a cascading impact to bring you more of that thing and helps set in motion and pave the way for future events to take place. Take possession of your goal fully in mind and it will eventually become your reality in body with enough sustained thought, gratitude, self-belief, and action.

We are like magnets, what we surround ourselves with, what we think about, what we focus on, we become. It's simple, what we think about we create and what we have gratitude for we get more of. Write down attributes of your most confident self and live as if you were already that person. You can do this for any goal you have, and it works wonders in making actionable steps more attainable. When we change our thoughts, we change what shows up in our reality. Prior to action, there must be a proceeding thought that sets the action in motion. Have you ever thought of something and then that exact thing appeared in your life some short time later? This is manifesting. It doesn't have to look like a miracle from heaven, it can be something very small like thinking about a song and then hearing the song play in the next few days, even if it's been 10 years since you last heard it. Manifesting could also be thinking about someone or having a dream about that person, and then unexpectedly receiving a call or text from them the next day. Manifesting takes many forms but can sometimes show up in surprising ways.

The reverse is also true, you can manifest and attract negative things into your life as well. Have you ever noticed people who are negative always seem to have something go wrong for them? Perhaps they are the complaining type that never shows appreciation for what they have, or they frequently talk badly or gossip about other people. You will find these people attract more negativity into their lives and it's not a coincidence. The universe acts like a mirror, and it will reflect at you what you are and what you think about, not what you merely want to be.

This is why it is so important to have gratitude for things before you have them and before they are a tangible reality. To make them a tangible reality you need to have gratitude for them as if they are already yours. Again, you need to take possession of it in mind before you can take possession of it in body. Once you do this and show gratitude for the confident person you are becoming you will begin to understand how to create the necessary action steps to become that person and that reality begins to be set in motion.

Being grateful for something that is intangible is one of the most impactful aspects of building your faith and remaining strong with your mindset and in your course of action. Believing that a higher version of yourself exists and displaying gratitude for already being that person — that is what it means to have true faith. The people who have strong faith and gratitude for things that are not yet tangible are the ones that reach their fullest potential in life and succeed in becoming the most confident versions of themselves.

To be grateful for something not yet present in your life you first need a great deal of clarity on details so you can begin to make that person as real as possible. Ask yourself what your most confident version of yourself looks like, dresses like, how they walk, talk, present themselves in meetings, who their friends are, where they spend their time, who they spend their time with, what they spend their time doing, what exercises do they do, what they do for recreation, what they do for work, how much they get paid for their work, etc. These are all leading questions that help you create actionable steps to become this desired person. We create our lifestyles and then our lifestyles create us in return so make it a point to create habits that lead to growth. Chances are the most confident version of you exercises, eats healthy, spends time doing work that they are passionate about, spends time with those they love, hangs out with a circle of friends that are growing, doesn't spend time gossiping, negotiates their salary, knows their worth, and knows how to walk into any room and command attention. Once you get clarity on who this person is and the characteristics and attributes they have, you can then begin to start the personal development journey necessary to become that person.

The Power of Action

Action steps can sometimes overwhelm people, they get bogged down by how many steps something will take or think a goal is too far out of reach and then not go for it as a result. However, any goal can be obtained with the right amount of clarity of thought followed by action. Once you have a visual representation in mind of your most confident self, start by doing one small thing that brings you a little closer to that person you want to be. For example, if your goal is to be heard during meetings then stop taking notes during meetings and acting like the scribe and start acting like the leader. Never go through one meeting without raising your hand or speaking up. Always make sure you establish your presence during meetings. Every time you put your head down to write something and take notes, you are not seen as a leader and every time your voice is not heard, you lose power.

    Start paying attention to confident people's body posture and take note of their shoulders especially. Confident people don't slouch or look hunched over during meetings, confident people have their shoulders pulled back, they stand tall, and they hold their body straight with good posture. Keep in mind, many experts agree that upwards of 90% of human communication is non-verbal, so being aware of your body posture and how you present yourself during meetings is very important in establishing confidence. "When there are inconsistencies between attitudes communicated verbally and posturally, the postural component should dominate in determining the total attitude that is inferred" ("How Much of Communication Is Nonverbal?", 2023). You are essentially telling your body you are more confident with what you are saying with your posture and the other person picks up on this communication as well. While showcasing confidence physically takes time, eventually with enough repetition and practice, both body and mind will start to act more confidently. Remember, for you to achieve the level of success you want in life, you must show confidence in both mind and body.

If you determine that the most confident version of yourself dresses a certain way, start small and tidy up your wardrobe to be more in line with that vision. You don't have to spend an exorbitant amount of money on an entirely new wardrobe but if you make small incremental adjustments, it can have a major impact on how you feel and how others perceive you. Don't pay attention to fashion trends or the latest fad, wear things that make you feel confident in your own skin, not anyone else's. If a particular color or style makes you feel confident, wear it. If you determine that your most confident self exercises more than you are currently exercising or eats healthier than you are currently eating, create a plan for incorporating manageably healthy habits into your lifestyle. For example, I feel my most confident self when I wear red lipstick, it's my superpower. When I put it on it makes me feel beautiful, so I made it a staple and now it is something I am known for. I also eat a balanced diet and exercise regularly because these habits also make me feel confident and beautiful. Wear things that make you feel confident, do activities that build confidence, and continually work to replace unbeneficial habits for healthy and empowering ones.

Even the smallest efforts can accumulate and make a profound difference over time. It could be as simple as improving 1% every day. If you are improving, it doesn't matter how small the incremental shift is. Of course, improving yourself by leaps and bounds is a great thing but it is not sustainable for most people, and this is a major reason why people give up. They often start something with the absolute best intentions in mind. They may eat healthy and exercise for a day or two and then give up and go back to their old habits afterwards. This is the reason why most diets fail and why New Year's resolutions are fleeting. People tend to have big goals and go all in and then lose motivation after a short burst of activity. The best thing you can do is to work on consistency and small incremental changes. We have all heard that consistency is key to attaining any goal, but it is very rarely put into practice. Remember that motivation is fleeting and does not last by itself unless you couple it with action and consistency.

If you improve 1% every day, by the end of a year you will be over 37X improved. You may even be unrecognizable. Just imagine this for a moment in your mind, what would the 37X improved version of you look like? The 37X improved version of yourself may be even more confident or successful than your original conception of your most confident self. Just imagine being this person mere months from now. Your life would change forever, you would never be the same again, you would be highly confident.

However, it takes work and dedication. You cannot expect to become more confident without putting in the work and without taking ownership. Through self-improvement you will begin to unlock and uncover the confident person you already are, but you first need to peel back the layers of self-doubt and fear that have been holding you back for years. The act of consistently improving and seeing incremental results creates a positive feedback loop. Each small success reinforces your belief in yourself and your ability to make progress. This cycle of positive reinforcement nurtures your confidence, providing the motivation to continue striving for growth and improvement.

Start by identifying one or two goals that you want to work towards and break them down into small, manageable steps that you can take each day. Here are some examples of small steps that are possible:

- Take a few minutes each day to learn something new, whether it's reading an article, watching a TED Talk, or listening to podcasts or audio books. This can help to expand your knowledge and skills and keep your mind engaged and active.

- Take a few minutes each day to reflect on the things that you are grateful for. This can help to shift your focus from what you don't have to what you do have and can improve your overall mood and well-being.
- Get at least 30 minutes of exercise each day, whether it's going for a walk, doing some yoga, or hitting the gym. Taking care of yourself is essential for personal growth and development. Even a small amount of exercise each day can have a significant impact on your physical and mental health.
- Make time each day to do something that brings you joy and relaxation, whether it's taking a bath, reading a book, or listening to music.
- Take a few minutes each day to connect with a friend, family member, or colleague, whether it's through a phone call, text message, or social media.
- Make meaningful connections with others to help improve your mood and boost your overall well-being.

- Avoid negativity in all forms including watching TV, movies, or news that depicts negative situations or events. Also do your best to avoid negative conversations as much as possible and when someone starts to talk negatively feel free to remove yourself from the exchange.

Remember, improving 1% every day doesn't have to be complicated or time-consuming. By making small, consistent changes each day, you can make steady progress towards your goals and become the best version of yourself. I set out to improve myself after I nearly ended my life on March 16, 2022. Every day from then on, I sought to improve myself by just 1%. This was a small enough amount that was achievable for me but still worked toward my goals. I began by removing my association with toxic friends, I stopped watching negative TV or movies, I cleaned up my diet, started a workout plan, reduced my alcohol, and refined sugar consumption, and I made a point to practice daily self-care, meditate, pray, and spend more quality time with my daughter.

The results were absolutely life changing. In less than

one year, I went from suicidal, overweight, depressed, and anxious to delivering a keynote speech, starting my book, scaling my business, and improving my relationship with my family and myself. When you practice this 1% rule and make it a lifestyle change and habit the results will be so incredible it will be nearly unbelievable. As incredible as it may sound, fifteen months after I nearly ended my life by suicide I was featured in Forbes Morocco as a thought leading entrepreneur, I secured a television interview with Fox News in Rochester New York, and landed my first TEDx talk in Nottinghamshire, England. My unstoppable confidence and unwavering sense of self-belief did not happen overnight but the bridge from failure to phenomenal success is much shorter than people generally perceive it to be and once you achieve this level of confidence, nothing seems out of scope or impossible.

A body in motion stays in motion so it is important to keep continuous action and focus on your confidence just as you would any other goal you have. Through action you naturally create momentum and progress begins to be inevitable because of your effort. This momentum continues to build your confidence levels and overtime it leads to more personal growth and increased self-belief. Just as a toddler when learning how to walk, falls and gets back up and continues without fear or doubt, so should you. As you take intentional steps towards improvement, you gain a deeper understanding of your strengths, weaknesses, and areas for development. This self-awareness allows you to make more informed decisions and trust yourself to navigate life's challenges with confidence.

Celebrate your wins and be proud of yourself when you take action. Don't worry that you have not reached your destination yet, celebrate the small victories and steps that you are taking as you progress in your journey. Celebrating your wins is important for building confidence because it reinforces a positive self-image, validates your efforts and accomplishments, and encourages further growth. It also reinforces positive behaviors and habits to be formed. By recognizing and rewarding your achievements, you strengthen the neural pathways associated with those behaviors, making them more likely to be repeated. This positive reinforcement fosters confidence in your ability to consistently achieve success and reinforces a growth mindset. It also trains your brain to look for the positive aspects of your experiences and cultivates a more optimistic outlook. This shift in mindset contributes to greater self-confidence and resilience in the face of challenges and if you couple this with continuous gratitude, forward progression will be inevitable. This increased self-belief translates into greater confidence, as you internalize the belief that you have what it takes to succeed.

The best result of daily self-improvement was that I began to love myself for the first time in my life. My self-confidence started to improve, and I felt myself awakening to possibility. I had more energy, more joy, and a zeal for life that I don't think I had ever had previously. Prior to this I never could have imagined that improving myself by just 1% would make such a difference but it was proof that consistency is the true key to success. If you can learn consistency, you can accomplish any goal, including building confidence. Through daily self-work, increasing healthy habits, and limiting exposure to negative environments your confidence will naturally begin to increase, as it did for me.

Practice these positive affirmations to develop gratitude for your future self so that you can begin to see your path clearly and stay on course. Say them as many times as it takes for you to appreciate your future reality so that you begin to believe that your goals will be possible for you:

1. I am grateful for the opportunities and possibilities that the future holds for me.
2. I am excited to see where my journey takes me, and I trust that the future holds many blessings for me.
3. I am thankful for the people who will come into my life in the future, and I am grateful for the connections we will make.
4. I am grateful for the knowledge and skills I will acquire in the future, and I am excited to use them to create a better life.
5. I am thankful for the adventures and experiences that the future will bring, and I am open to new opportunities.
6. I appreciate the personal growth and evolution that the future holds for me, and I am excited to see the person I will become.

7. I am grateful for the abundance of prosperity and success that the future holds for me.
8. I am thankful for the love and happiness that the future will bring, and I am open to receiving it with an open heart.
9. I am excited to fulfill my dreams and achieve my goals in the future, and I am grateful for the journey that will take me there.
10. I am grateful for the abundance of blessings and positivity that the future holds for me, and I am excited to embrace them with open arms.

Takeaways from this Chapter:

- *Embrace Self-Discovery*: Gratitude for the confident person you are becoming starts with acknowledging your journey of self-discovery. Embrace the process of learning more about yourself, your strengths, and your passions.

- *Celebrate Progress:* Recognize and celebrate the progress you've made so far on your path to becoming more confident. Each step, no matter how small, is a significant achievement worthy of appreciation.

- *Focus on Inner Growth*: Gratitude for your developing confidence goes beyond external achievements. Shift your focus to inner growth, such as improved self-belief, resilience, and the courage to face challenges.
- *Practice Positive Self-Talk:* Cultivate gratitude by engaging in positive self-talk. Replace self-doubt with affirmations that reinforce your growing confidence and remind yourself of your capabilities.
- *Visualize Success:* Use visualization techniques to see yourself as the confident person you aspire to be. Gratitude for this vision helps manifest your goals and increases your belief in your potential.
- *Learn from Setbacks:* View setbacks as opportunities for growth and learning. Gratitude allows you to find valuable lessons in challenges and use them to propel yourself further on your journey to confidence.
- *Surround Yourself with Support:* Express gratitude for the people who support and believe in your journey

to becoming more confident. Surrounding yourself with positive influences enhances your progress and fosters a sense of community.

- *Step Out of Your Comfort Zone:* Gratitude for your evolving confidence encourages you to embrace discomfort. Step out of your comfort zone and take on new challenges, knowing that every experience contributes to your growth.
- *Be Patient & Kind to Yourself:* Embrace gratitude for the person you are becoming, knowing that growth takes time. Be patient and kind to yourself throughout the process, avoiding self-criticism.

Lessons Learned from Having Gratitude for the Unstoppably Confident Person You Are Becoming:

- *A Resilient Mindset:* Gratitude instills a resilient mindset, allowing you to bounce back from setbacks and stay committed to your journey to confidence.
- *Unwavering Belief:* Gratitude for your growth cultivates an unwavering belief in your potential. It strengthens your self-trust and belief in your ability

to overcome challenges.

- *Living with Purpose:* Appreciating the person you are becoming brings a sense of purpose and direction to your life. You become more intentional in pursuing your goals and aspirations.
- *Inspiring Others:* Your gratitude for your developing confidence serves as an inspiration to those around you. It encourages others to embark on their journeys of self-improvement and growth.
- *Embracing Change:* Gratitude enables you to embrace change and adapt to new situations confidently. You become more open to opportunities and willing to explore new possibilities.
- *A Source of Motivation:* Being grateful for your evolving confidence fuels your motivation to keep moving forward. It reminds you of the progress you've made and encourages you to continue striving for personal growth.
- *Cultivating Optimism:* Gratitude fosters optimism, even in the face of challenges. You maintain a positive outlook, knowing that your confidence will

continue to flourish.

Embrace gratitude for the unstoppable confident person you are becoming, recognizing that your journey is as important as the destination. Each step forward, no matter how small, contributes to your growth and self-improvement. Celebrate your progress, learn from setbacks, and trust in your potential. Gratitude will be your constant companion on this transformative path, empowering you to embrace your confidence and face the world with courage and grace.

Your Turn:

1.) Describe in exact detail your most confident self:

2.) What steps are you willing to take to become this confident person?

3.) What are 10 things in your future that you already have gratitude for:

Chapter 4: Responsibility

Have Responsibility for your outcomes and an ownership mentality of your choices. Have responsibility for owning your power.

Highly confident people are charismatic and seem to have powers of gravitation — good things are always coming their way. They are like magnets and tend to get what they want, when they want it, and make no apologies for getting what they want. It almost seems like the universe is conspiring to deliver them everything they have ever dreamed of constantly.

We have all seen someone like this at some point in our lives and chances are, we told ourselves that that person must be perfect and unflawed and completely opposite of ourselves. I have been in meetings and seminars conducted by super confident people; they have all eyes and ears on them, and people can't help but listen to their every word. These people aren't gods, I assure you, they are as flawed and imperfect as you and I. They are not necessarily more qualified, more attractive, more educated, or smarter. They don't have less trauma or internal pain or suffering than anyone else. They are simply human beings who believe in themselves. They are confident by choice, through action and self-work. These confident people own their thoughts, actions, and choices and in no way believe life happens to them. They realize that they are the responsible party for their future outcomes and take a great deal of care to ensure that their good choices far outweigh their poor choices.

When I first heard someone say that human beings are the creators of our own realities, I had no idea what that meant. For many years, I thought that life happened to me and that I was a victim of my circumstances. I finally came to the realization that I was the creator of my future, and I was ultimately in charge of my actions, thoughts, and choices. By consciously choosing empowering thoughts, cultivating positive beliefs, and taking intentional actions, we can shape our reality and manifest the life we desire.

The best way to become the person you were meant to be is to have an ownership mindset and be responsible for overcoming your limitations. No matter who you were, who you are, or what circumstances you have had to overcome or are overcoming, have responsibility and take ownership of the outcomes. Failure to take ownership of our mindset is one of the biggest barriers you will face in gaining both confidence in yourself and overall success in your life. To become confident and step into your power, the best investment you can make is your mindset. Each of us are either the victim or the victor in our own stories so it is important to acknowledge very early on the importance of ownership and responsibility to ourselves.

If you experience a need for constant reassurance or outside validation from others, failure to give yourself credit for things you accomplish, compare yourself to other people, or tend to think of yourself as less than qualified, you may be experiencing feelings of self-doubt. If left unaddressed, these feelings can diminish your self-worth over time. Often when people experience self-doubt it prevents them from taking the necessary action needed to overcome a situation and make progress. Perhaps a fear of failure is preventing you from moving forward and is causing self-doubt. In your mind, you are already preparing to fail at something before you even try it and that works to keep you anchored right where you are. If this becomes a practice, it will inhibit growth potential long-term and lead to diminished confidence.

It is also common for people to suffer from a fear of success and think of what will be expected of them if they do succeed and what they will be responsible for if that happens. Self-sabotaging behavior and habits may start to form and, in a way, validate the limiting beliefs and self-doubt we are experiencing. I have seen this with many clients as they start their journeys of self-discovery and begin to peel back the layers of who they are as individuals and professionals. They begin to rise in their careers and then seemingly out of thin air they begin to fall backward into old habits or mindsets. This is self-sabotage. It is important to call these behaviors out within ourselves and address them. Whatever you do, don't permit them to take control. Remember, any setback is temporary, and failure is not fatal. However, growth is optional, and it is something that needs continual attention and nurturing to blossom.

Developing an ownership mindset is about taking responsibility for your life and your actions and seeing yourself as the driver of your own success. Your thoughts and beliefs shape your reality, so it's important to be aware of them and take responsibility for them. Notice any negative self-talk or limiting beliefs that may be holding you back and reframe them in a more positive and empowering way.

Imposter Syndrome

Do you ever feel that you don't belong or deserve to be in the role or position you are in, despite having all the necessary qualifications? Perhaps you feel as though people will begin to perceive you as a fraud or phony and eventually identify or expose you as such. You may feel as though people will begin to think of you as someone who is not qualified and judge you as a result. This is Imposter Syndrome.

The term was first coined in 1978 by two American psychologists, Pauline Clance and Suzanne Imes. "The term "impostor phenomenon" is used to designate an internal experience of intellectual phoniness that appears to be particularly prevalent and intense among a select sample of high achieving women. Certain early family dynamics and later introjection of societal sex-role stereotyping appear to contribute significantly to the development of the impostor phenomenon" (Clance P. R., & Imes, S. A. (1978).

Imposter syndrome disproportionally impacts women and minorities, but anyone can suffer from it. It's common even among high achieving individuals and can persist throughout an individual's life and result in lack of confidence and ultimately can lead someone to not enjoying the amount of success or confidence they are truly capable of achieving. These feelings are normal, and most people at some point in their lives experience them to some degree. However, they are not real and have no bearing on your abilities or who you are as an individual. Remember that no one will ever be as harsh on you as you are on yourself and very few people will expect more of you than you expect of yourself. Show yourself kindness and grace and when feelings of imposter syndrome begin to surface recognize them as such and power through with action.

When thoughts of imposter syndrome begin to creep in, make a list or say out loud some things that contradict the feelings of imposter syndrome. Listing your achievements, accomplishments, and things you are doing right can have a powerful impact on combatting imposter syndrome. It is important to have ownership of your speech and thoughts. It is normal for negativity to surface for anyone but as soon as it does, it's your responsibility to reframe it into something growth oriented instead of something limiting.

Overcoming these insecurities can be challenging, but there are strategies you can use to alleviate imposter syndrome when it starts to creep in.

- Understand that imposter syndrome is a common experience and that many successful people struggle with it. This will help you feel less alone and more validated in your experiences.
- Challenge negative self-talk and reframe it with positive self-talk. We'll discuss this further in the next section.
- Remind yourself of your accomplishments, skills, and positive qualities. Write down your achievements and read them when you need a confidence boost.
- Talk to trusted friends, family members, or colleagues about your feelings of imposter syndrome. They may

be able to provide reassurance, support, and perspective that can help you feel more confident.

- Recognize that everyone has weaknesses, and it's okay to make mistakes or not know everything.
- Practice self-care: taking care of yourself is essential for building confidence and overcoming imposter syndrome. Engage in activities that make you feel good, such as exercise, meditation, or hobbies. Prioritize your mental health and well-being and make time for self-care activities that help you relax and recharge.

Imposter syndrome is a process that requires self-awareness, self-compassion, and support from others. Reframing negative self-talk, focusing on strengths, seeking support, and practicing self-care can all help build confidence and overcome feelings of imposter syndrome. Remember that it's okay to make mistakes, and that your accomplishments are valid and worthy of recognition.

Negative Self-Talk

"We produce up to 50,000 thoughts a day and 70% to 80% of those are negative. This translates into 40,000 negative thoughts a day that need managing and filtering" (Lambersky, 2013). It is important to note that this data is based on the average person, so this is completely normal to have negative thoughts. However, these numbers are understandably compounded for people who are suffering from a lack of confidence. Imagine the day when your 40,000 negative thoughts are replaced with 40,000 empowering ones. By understanding the prevalence of negative thoughts, we can identify recurring patterns or triggers that lead to them. This insight allows us to address underlying issues and take proactive steps to avoid or cope with situations that tend to bring about negative thinking.

Do any of these phrases sound familiar to you?
- I am a failure.
- I don't belong.
- I am not good at anything.
- I can never do anything right.
- I'll never be able to accomplish that.
- I'm a screw up and I'll never be successful.
- I am not smart, talented, or attractive enough.

Our subconscious minds pick up on speech and thoughts and over time we begin to believe what we tell ourselves. To get started with breaking the cycle of negative self-talk you first must acknowledge it and become aware of it when it happens. Without this awareness, you will repeat the cycle again and again until it becomes a fixed belief in your mind. It is important to begin to reframe the speech and thought patterns you have about yourself into positive, growth minded phrases instead of limiting phrases. The subconscious mind is highly receptive and can absorb and internalize the messages it receives. Negative or self-limiting speech can shape our subconscious beliefs, influencing our thoughts, emotions, and actions. By guarding our speech and choosing words that are positive, empowering, and aligned with our goals and values, we can create a nurturing environment for our subconscious mind, fostering a positive mindset and supporting our personal growth and well-being.

By providing clear and positive instructions, you can harness the potential of your subconscious mind to work towards your goals and desires. This practice is beneficial because the subconscious mind operates on autopilot, influencing your actions and decisions even without conscious awareness. By giving it specific directives aligned with what you want to achieve, you program it to seek opportunities, solutions, and resources that support your desired outcomes. This focused programming of the subconscious mind helps align your thoughts, beliefs, and actions with your goals, increasing your chances of success and creating a more positive and fulfilling life experience.

Give your subconscious mind definite orders but keep it positive, goal-focused, and growth-oriented. Write out a clear statement for your subconscious mind to act upon and set a deadline for achieving that statement. Clearly articulate your goal in specific and measurable terms. The more specific and well-defined your goal is, the easier it becomes for your subconscious mind to comprehend and work towards it. Construct positive and affirming statements that reflect the successful attainment of your goal. Repeat these affirmations to yourself regularly, both verbally and in writing. For example, if your goal is to become more confident, you can say affirmations like, "I am worthy, confident, capable, and deserving of success." Write a statement that will serve as instructions and programming to your subconscious mind.

Example:

> "I am fully committed to developing unstoppable confidence and embracing an ownership mindset. By [insert date, e.g., June 30th, 2025], I will have cultivated unwavering confidence and a strong sense of responsibility in all aspects of my life, and I will feel powerful and purposeful.
>
> I trust in the immense power of my subconscious mind to rewire my beliefs and thought patterns. I trust in my mind's ability to let go of any self-doubt and limiting beliefs that are holding me back from reaching my full potential. I actively replace negative beliefs and thoughts with empowering ones that reinforce my abilities and worthiness of success.
>
> Throughout this journey, I am grateful for the unwavering support and assistance from my mind, body, and spirit. I acknowledge that I have the power to shape my

life and confidently pursue my dreams.
I express deep appreciation for my transforming mindset and outlook on life. My life is filled with confidence, purpose, and a sense of responsibility that enables continued growth and progress.
Thank you, subconscious mind, for making this transformation possible. By [insert date], I will have developed unstoppable confidence and embraced a mindset that knows no limits, creating a life that is filled with success, self-assurance, and fulfillment.
I am excited to witness the remarkable changes that are happening and that will continue to happen in my life."

Consistency is key when giving orders to your subconscious mind. Repeat your affirmations and visualization exercises regularly, preferably daily. Consistent repetition reinforces the programming and helps align your conscious and subconscious mind towards your desired outcome. Memorize the statement for the specific goal you want to achieve and say it throughout the day and again before going to bed. When you repeat your statement, believe that your subconscious mind is acting on it. See yourself already in possession of what your statement calls for. Close your statement by professing profound gratitude for having received what you asked for. Before repeating your statement, focus on feelings of joy, gratitude, and love to help you achieve a high vibrational state. Know that your request will be fulfilled and have faith that everything you want is on its way to you. It is very important to program our minds with messages and images of confidence and success reinforced with positivity. While the subconscious mind is a powerful ally, it's important to remember that action is necessary to achieve your goals. Break down your goal into smaller, actionable steps and actively work towards them. By taking inspired action, you provide tangible evidence to your subconscious mind that you are committed to achieving your goal.

It is important to remember that these principles extend beyond ourselves. Always be mindful of your speech and avoid talking negatively about other people. Our subconscious mind picks up on all of it. Become aware of when you engage in negative self-talk or gossip. Try to identify the triggers or situations that lead to these behaviors. Once you have identified them, you can work on developing alternative, more positive responses. Focus on positive or neutral topics of conversation. Surround yourself with positive people who lift you up and encourage positive thinking. Similarly, try to be a positive influence on others by offering words of encouragement. Stopping negative self-talk and gossip requires self-awareness, positive thinking, and a commitment to positivity. By replacing negative thoughts with positive ones, cultivating gratitude, avoiding gossip, and encouraging positivity in yourself and others, you can create a more positive mindset and improve your relationships with others and yourself.

Limiting Beliefs

Limiting beliefs are like negative self-talk and imposter syndrome. You may say phrases like:

- I can't.
- I don't deserve this.
- I'm not good enough.
- I'm not smart enough.

- I'm not qualified enough.
- I'm not attractive enough.
- I'm too old or too young to accomplish that goal.
- I've messed up too many times and I am a failure.
- I don't have the time or money to invest in myself.

Each one of these phrases effectively gives you permission to stop trying and inhibits growth. Stop accepting that narrative. Instead of saying something like, "I **CAN'T** afford that," start saying growth-oriented phrases like, "**HOW** can I afford that?" Lead with a question, instead of an absolute statement. Instead of, "I am **NOT** confident enough to do that," try saying, "**HOW** can I become confident enough to do that?"

Limiting beliefs in your mind will lead to limited outcomes and you will begin to believe and accept them as factual. Reframe your beliefs into opportunities for growth and potential instead.

Limiting beliefs may also surface through comparison of other people. Someone in your same field may be further ahead of you and seemingly more successful, more wealthy, happier, or healthier. Perhaps you have compared yourself to that person, and it has discouraged you. You may believe that the other person is more talented than you, more attractive than you, or more connected than you and begin to tell yourself that there is no way you could be like them so why try? Comparing ourselves to others eradicates confidence, joy, and limits potential. There is no shortage of opportunity for any person who is doing something they love and are naturally gifted at. We will discuss purpose in a later chapter, but in the meantime, take note of these limiting feelings you have and acknowledge them for what they are — something not rooted in reality. A confident person must take responsibility for the thoughts or beliefs that work to limit their potential and diminish their confidence.

Practice these positive affirmations to develop an ownership mindset centered around responsibility over your thought process and actions. Say them as many times as necessary to progress your thinking and change your patterns:

1. I take full responsibility for my life and my actions, and I am committed to creating a better future for myself.
2. I am in control of my thoughts and emotions, and I

choose to focus on positivity and growth.

3. I can make positive changes in my life, and I am committed to acting towards my goals.
4. I take ownership of my mistakes and learn from them, using them as opportunities for growth and self-improvement.
5. I am accountable for my choices, and I make decisions that align with my values and goals.
6. I am responsible for my own happiness and well-being, and I take care of myself both physically and mentally.
7. I am proactive and take initiative in pursuing my dreams and goals, rather than waiting for opportunities to come to me.
8. I am committed to continuous learning and personal growth, and I take action to develop my skills and knowledge.
9. I am grateful for the opportunities and resources available to me, and I take full advantage of them.
10. I am confident in my ability to overcome obstacles and challenges, and I use them as opportunities to develop my resilience and strength.

Takeaways from this Chapter:

- *Own Your Actions:* Developing a responsibility mindset starts with taking ownership of your choices and actions. Acknowledge that you have control over your decisions and their consequences, which empowers you to steer your life in a positive direction.
- *Learn from Mistakes:* Embrace responsibility for your mistakes and view them as opportunities for growth. When you take accountability for your errors, you can learn valuable lessons and make better decisions in the future.
- *Set Clear Goals:* Establish clear and achievable goals for yourself. A responsibility mindset involves setting intentions and taking proactive steps to achieve them, leading to increased confidence as you make progress.
- *Be Reliable & Trustworthy:* Consistently follow through on your commitments and promises. Being reliable and trustworthy builds self-assurance as you prove to yourself and others that you can be counted on.
- *Avoid Blame & Excuses:* Shift away from blaming others or making excuses for unfavorable outcomes. Instead,

focus on finding solutions and adapting to challenges, which strengthens your sense of responsibility and self-assurance.

- *Take Initiative:* Cultivate a sense of responsibility by taking initiative and seeking opportunities for personal and professional growth. Stepping out of your comfort zone and embracing new challenges fosters self-confidence.
- *Seek Feedback:* Be open to feedback and constructive criticism. A responsibility mindset involves using feedback as a tool for improvement rather than taking it personally, leading to continuous self-development.
- *Celebrate Achievements:* Acknowledge and celebrate your achievements, both big and small. Recognizing your successes reinforces a positive sense of responsibility for your accomplishments and boosts your confidence.

Lessons Learned from Developing a Responsibility Mindset for Confidence:

- *Empowerment through Accountability:* A responsibility mindset empowers you to take charge of your life.

When you take responsibility for your choices, you regain control over your destiny and become the driver of your success.

- *Building Trust in Yourself:* Assuming responsibility builds trust in your abilities. As you consistently fulfill your commitments, you develop confidence in your capability to handle various situations.
- *Resilience in Adversity:* A responsibility mindset fosters resilience in the face of challenges. Rather than feeling helpless, you focus on finding solutions and maintaining confidence in your problem-solving skills.
- *Increased Self-Worth:* Embracing responsibility cultivates a stronger sense of self-worth. You recognize your value and contributions, which bolsters your self-esteem and overall confidence.
- *Leadership & Influence:* Responsibility and confidence go hand in hand with effective leadership. When you take responsibility for your actions, others perceive you as reliable and influential.
- *A Growth-Oriented Outlook:* A responsibility mindset encourages a growth-oriented outlook on life. You

embrace change, continuous learning, and self-improvement, leading to increased confidence in your adaptability.

- *Creating Positive Impact:* Taking responsibility allows you to create a positive impact on your life and the lives of others. Confidence in your ability to make a difference fuels your determination to contribute meaningfully.

By developing a responsibility mindset, you lay the foundation for a confident and purposeful life. Embrace accountability for your actions, learn from mistakes, and set clear goals to empower yourself on your journey of personal growth. Remember that confidence stems from taking ownership of your life and actively shaping it into one filled with purpose and achievement.

Your Turn:

What steps do you need to take today to reduce or eliminate negative speech, gossiping and limiting beliefs?

What about you contradicts negative thoughts or beliefs you sometimes have about yourself? Brag about yourself!

Chapter 5: Action

Act as if you are already the most confident version of yourself and don't let anything stop you. Confidence is a daily practice and habit. It takes consistent action, daily self-work, and continual progress in the right direction.

No amount of thought can replace action so if you want to create real, tangible change in your life, you must act. My life began to open for me when I realized that change starts with a willingness to step outside my comfort zone and challenge my self-imposed limitations. I began by taking small but intentional steps like joining networking events, appearing on podcasts, hosting webinars, posting informative or motivational videos of myself on social media, and embracing opportunities for growth. Each action, no matter how daunting, helped me build momentum and proved to myself that I was capable. With each success, my confidence grew, and I found myself eagerly seeking new challenges. Through consistent effort and a commitment to personal growth, I discovered that confidence is developed and magnified through actions and mindset. With each action we take, whether big or small, we prove to ourselves that we are capable. We demonstrate that we have the power to make things happen, to overcome obstacles, and to achieve our goals. Every step forward, even if it results in failure or setbacks, provides valuable lessons and insights that fuel our growth. Today, I stand tall, proud of the person I have become, knowing that I have the power to overcome any obstacle and live a life filled with self-assurance and fulfillment.

Do not sit and dwell on your thoughts or visions with the hope that your life improves and gets better. The best and most effective way to remove self-doubt is through action. Don't wait to become confident to progress with your goals but instead gain confidence through your activity. The best determinator of future success is present action so you must put in the work to see improvement. Action is often a step that goes unaccounted for by most individuals which inevitably leads to failure and frustration. No amount of thinking will result in manifesting, you need to put in the work to see the results. Many people get caught up in the "how" and often forget to focus on the "now" and as a result have failure to act. When you think about action, I don't want you to focus on the past or the future, I only want you to focus on your present action because that is the only thing you have control of.

The best way to keep a present mind is through continual practices of gratitude as stated in chapter one and throughout this entire book because gratitude is the foundation for confidence, success, and general fulfillment in life. Focus on what you have control of and don't focus on anything that you can't change. The only thing you can control in your life is your present action. No amount of dwelling on the past or ruminating about the future will create action so there is no point in wasting your time or energy on either.

Goal Setting

It is important to have a clear vision and strategy in place to enable successful action and progress. Action in the absence of clarity of vision and strategy can lead to getting off course and making decisions that are not aligned with your goals. There are no rewards for producing a lot of fruitless action that leads you to going 100 miles in the wrong direction. When you act without a clear sense of direction, you may end up wasting time, resources, and energy on activities that do not move you closer to your desired outcome. Having a vision and strategy in place helps you stay focused on what truly matters and ensures that your actions are purposeful and intentional. A clear vision provides a sense of direction and purpose, while a strategy outlines the specific steps and resources needed to achieve that vision. When you have a clear vision and strategy, you can make decisions and take actions that are aligned with your goals and values. You can also stay flexible and adapt your strategy as needed based on feedback and new information. By taking the time to develop a vision and strategy, you can set yourself up for success and avoid getting off course.

The 1-in-60 Rule

To illustrate my point, in aviation, there is a rule of thumb that pilots use as a guide. The rule of thumb is called the 1 in 60 rule. If a plane is flying one degree off course and it travels 60 nautical miles, it will end up being 1 mile off course. This is proportionate to every degree that the plane is off course, and it is easy to understand how quickly a small change or shift can impact the trajectory of the plane's outcome. Now, think about how quickly a plane can travel 60 miles and that puts it even more into perspective. Instead of landing the plane on the landing strip there may be nowhere to land the plane and it could lead to a disastrous outcome. The same is true with decision making in life, for you to have the most effective outcome, you need to couple action with intention and strategy while having responsibility for the outcome.

In life, it doesn't require a great deal of straying to get off course very quickly. One or two degrees can change where you go in life, just as it changes the direction the plane travels. In terms of personal life and choices, the one in 60 rule can be a useful principle to apply in decision-making and goal setting. By regularly checking in with ourselves and our progress, we can ensure that we stay on track and avoid getting off course. For example, if we have a long-term goal, such as losing weight, becoming confident, or saving money, we can apply the one in 60 rule by regularly checking in on our progress and adjusting as needed. This might involve setting smaller milestones along the way, such as losing a certain amount of weight each month or saving a certain amount of money each paycheck and monitoring your progress towards these milestones on a regular basis.

Similarly, in our daily lives, we can apply the one in 60 rule by taking regular breaks to check in with ourselves and our priorities. This might involve taking a few minutes each day to reflect on our progress and adjust our focus as needed or taking a few minutes each day to practice self-care and prioritize our well-being. Overall, the one in 60 rule emphasizes the importance of regular check-ins and cross-checks, both in aviation and in our personal lives. By staying aware of our surroundings, our goals, and our progress, we can ensure that we stay on course and reach our destinations safely and successfully. The best thing you can do is to have strategy and think with clarity before creating a lot of action that gets you off course and wastes your time. This same logical thinking can be applied to any aspect of your life or business. Plan out a strategy to become more confident just as you would map out anything else. The clearer you are on your plans, the simpler it will be to achieve them.

Concrete Steps Toward Becoming Your Most Confident Self

In the previous chapters, we discussed the importance of visualizing your most confident self. Armed with a clarity of that vision, I want you to take some time to think about the action steps that are required for you to become that person. You must act on the vision so that you don't slip back into old habits, behaviors, mindsets, or ways of doing things. Form actionable steps to accomplish your goals to lay the foundation and framework necessary to become that person. Keep in mind, that all actionable steps that lead to you to be the most confident version of yourself require self-work and self-improvement initiatives. No amount of thinking will replace any amount of doing, so it is time to get to work and take ownership and responsibility of your confidence through action.

Start by identifying what you want to achieve and why. Make sure your goals align with your values and aspirations.

Identifying what you want to achieve requires self-reflection and introspection. This process helps you gain a deeper understanding of your strengths, weaknesses, passions, and values. As you become more self-aware, you can align your goals with your natural abilities and interests, increasing the likelihood of success. This self-awareness contributes to building authentic confidence based on a genuine understanding of yourself. By understanding your goals and reasons, you can develop a strong sense of self-belief and empower yourself to take meaningful steps toward success.

Write down your goals and be as specific as possible. Writing down your goals is important because it can help clarify your vision and provide a clear roadmap for achieving your desired outcomes. When you write down your goals, you are making a commitment to yourself to act towards achieving them. This can be a powerful motivator and can help you stay focused on what you want to accomplish. Writing down your goals also helps you to be more specific and detailed about what you want to achieve. This level of detail can help you break down your goals into smaller, more manageable tasks, which can make them feel less overwhelming. When you have a clear plan of action, it's easier to take steps towards achieving your goals, rather than feeling lost or unsure of what to do next. In addition to providing clarity and structure, writing down your goals can also help hold you accountable. When you put your goals in writing, you are creating a tangible reminder of what you want to achieve. This can help you stay focused on your goals and make it more difficult to ignore them or put them off. Moreover, writing down your goals can help you track your progress and celebrate your successes. You can use your written goals to create a plan for achieving them, and then track your progress as you complete each task. This can be a powerful tool for building confidence and motivation, as you see yourself making progress towards achieving your goals.

Set deadlines for each step and prioritize your actions. When you have a specific timeframe within which to accomplish a task or goal, it increases your motivation to get started and maintain momentum. This sense of urgency pushes you to prioritize your actions and avoid procrastination, resulting in increased productivity and a greater sense of accomplishment. Deadlines provide a sense of accountability and hold you responsible for meeting your objectives. When you set a deadline, you make a commitment to yourself or others to accomplish a specific task or goal within a given timeframe. This commitment fosters a stronger sense of responsibility and encourages you to follow through with the necessary actions. By meeting your deadlines consistently, you build a sense of trust in your ability to deliver on your promises, thus enhancing your confidence.

Focus your attention on your goals by eliminating any distractions that may be getting in your way. This could involve setting boundaries with others, turning off notifications on your phone, or creating a dedicated workspace. Limiting distractions requires self-discipline and self-control. It involves resisting the urge to engage in activities or behaviors that divert your attention from your goals. By practicing self-discipline and intentionally avoiding distractions, you strengthen your ability to stay committed to your objectives. This enhanced self-discipline contributes to building confidence as you develop a sense of mastery over your actions and choices. When you have uninterrupted time and space, you can evaluate your progress, strengths, and areas for improvement more effectively. This self-reflection aids in building confidence as you gain a clearer understanding of your capabilities and areas where you can further develop and grow.

Surround yourself with people who support your goals and can provide guidance and encouragement along the way. This could involve joining a support group, hiring a coach or mentor, or simply confiding in trusted friends and family members. There is no shame in going to therapy or meeting with a coach to help you out of a situation. The most successful people I have ever met have one or more coaches, including myself.

Professional athletes stay on top by having coaches that continually push them to achieve new heights and break records so why would you think that having a coach or therapist is something that is not needed for you? The most successful professionals and athletes are trained by the best coaches and surround themselves with the best people who are continually growing and moving towards something greater. This is how you remain at the top of your game and amplify your confidence. If your goal is to achieve confidence but you have blockages in your way from unresolved past wounds than the best thing you can do for yourself is to talk to someone who is trained that can help you resolve them. For example, if you are continually leaving money or opportunities on the table every year because you lack the confidence to ask for what you want, a few therapy or coaching sessions could very well give you a return on your investment quickly. Perhaps you are staying in toxic relationships or environments because of a lack of confidence to move forward. In either scenario you are wasting time, and no one can afford to waste time not feeling confident and powerful so take the necessary action steps needed to make your goals possible. Stop being the one holding yourself back, you are more powerful than you can possibly imagine but only if you allow yourself to be helped. Act and start immediately.

Set clear goals, develop an action plan, eliminate distractions, visualize success, reflect on why gaining confidence is important to you, and seek support. These steps will help you achieve the clarity you need to attain your goals, reach your full potential, and become incredibly confident.

Identifying Reasons for Inaction

People may fail to act for a variety of reasons. You may be afraid of failure or the consequences of acting, such as making a mistake, being rejected, or facing criticism. This fear can be paralyzing and prevent you from taking any action at all. You may feel like you need to have everything perfect before acting, which can lead to procrastination and inactivity. Perhaps you lack the motivation or energy to act, particularly if the task at hand feels overwhelming or uninteresting, this is common but not a reason to sit back. Don't doubt your abilities or feel like they're not qualified. This lack of confidence can hold you back from pursuing your goals. If you have the desire to do something and there is a seed of confidence within you, then you have all the power and potential to accomplish that thing. While it is common to feel overwhelmed by the sheer number of tasks or responsibilities we have in life, when we begin to feel this way, take a moment, and reflect with gratitude for how far you have come in your process and reframe it once again with an ownership and responsibility mindset. If you are feeling overwhelmed, go back through the steps outlined in this book to recenter your thoughts. Only focus on things that you can control and fixate your intentions and actions toward the controllable factors in your life.

Recognize the mental barriers that are causing your inaction and address them when they arise. Observe your internal dialogue, identify recurring negative thoughts or self-doubt, and reflect on any deep-rooted fears or limiting beliefs that may be holding you back. This will help you overcome inaction and take steps towards achieving confidence. Know that each action step you take will bring you closer to your desired outcomes and a life of fulfillment.

Practice these positive affirmations to make action a priority in your life. Say them as many times as necessary to motivate you and keep you focused on your goals and desired outcomes:

1. I can achieve my goals and I am willing to act towards my dreams.
2. I am proactive and take initiative in pursuing my dreams and goals.
3. I am confident in my abilities to succeed, and I act

with determination.

4. I am committed to taking consistent and purposeful action towards my goals every day.
5. I am resourceful and find creative solutions to any obstacles that may arise in my path.
6. I am fearless in the face of challenges, and I trust in my ability to overcome them.
7. I am excited to take bold and courageous action towards my dreams and goals.
8. I am disciplined and committed to the daily habits and actions that will lead to my success.
9. I am grateful for the opportunities and resources available to me, and I take full advantage of them to achieve my goals.
10. I am focused on my vision and take intentional action towards creating the life I desire.

Takeaways from this Chapter:

- *Step Outside Your Comfort Zone:* Taking action requires pushing past your comfort zone. Embrace discomfort as a stepping stone to growth and confidence, as every small step you take will lead you closer to becoming your most confident self.

- *Set Specific Goals:* Define clear and measurable goals for building confidence. Break these goals into manageable steps and take consistent action towards achieving them.
- *Practice Self-Compassion:* Be kind to yourself throughout the process. Acknowledge that building confidence is a journey, and setbacks are natural. Treat yourself with the same kindness and understanding you would offer a close friend.
- *Challenge Negative Thoughts:* Identify and challenge negative self-talk that undermines your confidence. Replace these thoughts with positive affirmations and empowering beliefs about yourself and your capabilities.
- *Embrace a Growth Mindset:* Cultivate a growth mindset, believing that your abilities can be developed through effort and perseverance. This mindset encourages you to view challenges as opportunities for learning and growth.
- *Visualize Your Confident Self:* Practice visualization

techniques to see yourself as your most confident version. Visualizing success helps create a strong mental image of your potential and fosters belief in your abilities.

- *Seek Support & Encouragement:* Surround yourself with supportive and encouraging individuals who believe in your journey. Share your aspirations with trusted friends, family, or mentors who can provide valuable guidance and support.
- *Take Incremental Steps:* Building confidence doesn't happen overnight. Take small, consistent steps towards your goals, celebrating each achievement along the way, no matter how minor it may seem.

Lessons Learned from Taking Action to Become Your Most Confident Self:

- *Courage Breeds Confidence:* Taking action requires courage, and every step you take builds confidence. Embrace the bravery needed to pursue your goals and recognize that each step forward strengthens your self-assurance.

- *Embrace Setbacks as Learning Opportunities:* Setbacks are a natural part of any growth journey. Instead of being discouraged, use them as opportunities to learn, adjust, and keep moving forward.

- *Confidence Grows with Experience:* As you take action and gain experience, your confidence naturally grows. Embrace each experience as an opportunity to learn and improve, leading to greater self-assurance.

- *Consistency is Key:* Consistent action is essential for building confidence. Regularly challenge yourself, and over time, you'll notice a significant transformation in your self-belief and abilities.

- *Self-Belief Attracts Opportunities:* As you become more confident in yourself, you'll notice that opportunities start to present themselves. People are drawn to confidence, and your belief in yourself will open doors you never thought possible.

- *Confidence is an Ongoing Journey:* Building confidence is not a destination; it's an ongoing journey. Embrace the process and continue striving for growth, as confidence evolves along with you.

- *Confidence Inspires Others:* As you take action and become more confident, you inspire others to do the same. Your journey can serve as a positive example, motivating those around you to pursue their own self-improvement.

Taking action to become your most confident self is a transformative process that requires dedication and perseverance. Embrace discomfort, set specific goals, and challenge negative thoughts. With consistency and self-compassion, you'll witness incredible personal growth and find yourself on a journey towards becoming the most confident version of yourself. Remember that confidence is a skill that can be developed through intentional action and a belief in your own potential.

Your Turn:

1.) Identify what you want to achieve and why, be as detailed as possible.

2.) What is your deadline for achieving these goals?

3.) What distractions do you need to remove from your life to help you achieve your goals?

4.) What are 10 action steps you can take today to act on your goals?

Chapter 6: Sight

Keep your Sights, your thoughts, and your vision closely guarded. Never let fear, limiting beliefs, or self-doubt detract you from your vision or your goals.

Embarking on a journey without a clear sight is like navigating through a dense fog; only with clarity of sight can we chart a course towards our goals and illuminate the path to success. Clarity of sight acts as the compass that not only guides your steps but ignites the unwavering determination necessary to transform mere goals into remarkable achievements. While sight and visualization share a connection through the act of perceiving images, they are not the same.

Sight refers to the physical ability to perceive visual stimuli through the eyes, while visualization involves mentally creating or recreating images in one's mind's eye. Sight relies on the external world, capturing what is directly in front of us, while visualization taps into our imagination, allowing us to conjure up images that may not exist in the present moment. Visualization can be a powerful tool for manifesting goals, practicing skills, and fostering creativity, whereas sight is the direct reception of visual information from the surrounding environment. Building confidence requires you to have clarity of your goals in a physical sense through sight as well as within your mind through visualization. Both sight and visualization build on and complement each other.

When you have a clear vision of what you want to achieve and who you want to become, you need to anchor that vision in your mind. Anchoring your vision will help you stay focused and motivated, even during times of difficulty or hardship. Seeing your goal clearly in your mind as well as physically can help you develop a sense of purpose, and this can provide the drive you need to act towards achieving that goal. Anchoring your vision means creating a mental image of what it will look and feel like to achieve your objective and it serves as a constant reminder of what you are working towards. When you anchor your vision and keep your sights clear, it guides your actions and decisions in a way that supports the realization of your vision. This can include imagining the result, as well as the steps you need to take along the way. When you have a clear vision of your goal and anchor it in your mind, you are better able to maintain your focus and stay motivated, even when faced with obstacles or setbacks. When you can see yourself achieving your goal, and you believe in your ability to make it happen, you are more likely to stay optimistic and persistent, even when times get tough. As Marian Wright Edelman once said, "You can't be what you can't see" so visualize who you want to become and believe that you can transform into that person.

In sports, visualization is a powerful tool for athletes because it can help them improve their performance and increase their chances of winning. Visualization involves creating a mental image of a desired outcome, and athletes can use this technique to mentally rehearse their movements and actions. By visualizing themselves succeeding, athletes can develop a sense of confidence and belief in their ability to perform well. One of the main benefits of visualization for athletes is that it allows them to mentally rehearse their movements and actions. When athletes visualize themselves performing well, it can help them improve their muscle memory and overall performance. This can be especially helpful in sports where precision and timing are crucial, such as gymnastics or diving. By mentally rehearsing their movements, athletes can become more familiar with the sequence of actions required to execute a skill, and this can help them perform more confidently and accurately during competition.

In addition to improving performance and goal setting, visualization can also help reduce anxiety and stress. By creating a sense of familiarity with the task at hand, visualization can help you feel more comfortable and confident in your abilities. This can be especially helpful in high-pressure situations, such as delivering a presentation at work, during a competition, completing a major project, or closing a deal with a client. When athletes feel calm and focused, they are more likely to perform at their best and increase their chances of winning. However, visualization can be done by anyone, not just athletes. Confidence is like a sport in many ways. Confidence requires constant visualization, positive self-talk, consistent practice, an ownership mindset, and intense drive to become better. However, in the game of confidence, you are not playing against any other person. Your only competition is yourself and your goal is to become better and more confident than who you were yesterday.

Tools for Cultivating Sight

A great way to anchor your sight is to create a vision board or something comparable. Vision boards provide a visual representation of your goals, dreams, and aspirations. A vision board is a collage of images, words, and symbols that depict the things you want to manifest or achieve in your life. The purpose of a vision board is to serve as a visual reminder and source of inspiration for your desired outcomes. By regularly looking at your vision board, you reinforce positive thoughts and intentions, keeping your goals at the forefront of your mind. As simple as it sounds, there is so much power in visual elements when you are focusing on a goal, especially if your goal is to increase your confidence.

While I was still at my corporate job, about two months prior to giving my notice I created my first vision board. At that time, I had no concept of what a vision board really was or why it was important. I even had to look it up online to make sure I understood the concept clearly. I went to work and purchased a tri-fold poster board and began looking up images of what I imagined my dream life to be. A vision board is a powerful tool that can help you bring your dream to reality by providing a tangible representation of your goals and aspirations. It is a visual representation of the things you want to achieve, the things you want to have, and the things you want to experience. One of the main ways that a vision board can help you bring your dream to reality is by keeping your goals and aspirations at the forefront of your mind. When you create a vision board, you are essentially creating a visual reminder of the things you want to achieve. By looking at your vision board regularly, you can stay focused on your goals and keep them top of mind.

Another way that a vision board can help you bring your dream to reality is by helping you clarify and refine your goals. When you create a vision board, you are forced to articulate your goals and aspirations in a concrete and specific way. This process of clarifying your goals can help you to identify the specific actions you need to take to achieve them. Vision boards can help you bring your dream to reality by increasing your motivation and commitment. When you have a visual reminder of your goals and aspirations, you are more likely to stay motivated and committed to achieving them. This can help you to push through obstacles and challenges that might otherwise derail your progress. Overall, a vision board can be a powerful tool for bringing your dreams to reality. By keeping your goals top of mind, clarifying your aspirations, and increasing your motivation and commitment, a vision board can help you to stay focused and on track as you work towards achieving your goals.

My first vision board included pictures of my dream home, vacations, fancy cars, a happy family, and a healthier body. I began to identify visual elements of what I wanted my life to look and feel like for the first time in my life. Achieving clarity of what success looked like to me and how I defined it was an important step for me to take to achieve those outcomes. In the center of the board, I chose an image that was surprising to me at the time, but it called to me. Directly in the center was a picture of a confident lady delivering a keynote speech to a large audience and then right below was a picture of a microphone on a stand ready for me to walk up to it and start talking. Keep in mind, at this time I had nearly zero self-esteem, and I was terrified to speak up, even during company zoom calls and meetings.

When I quit my job two months later, the board along with some other personal items got thrown away. However, I had the vision firmly fixed into my mind and I can still see it in detail until this day. Several months went by and I was consumed with trying to grow my company, not giving my vision board much thought. About six months later I meant a professional speaker on LinkedIn, and we hit it off instantly. I casually told him about the vision board I had created those months prior and mentioned that I thought I was meant to get into the industry in some way. When you align with your purpose, things begin to move toward you just as the law of gravitation. You become attracted towards certain things, and the universe begins to conspire to give you everything you need for you to accomplish your purpose, including increased confidence in yourself, your skillset, and your abilities. He mentioned to me that there were programs out there to help anyone become a professional speaker and if that is something I wanted, he would help me. Eight months after initially creating my vision board and less than four months after that conversation, I delivered my first keynote speech, and my life was forever changed as a result.

After you get clarity on what you want, turn your vision board into practical real-life application. For example, when I began practicing for my TEDx talk I purchased a small red circular area rug to rehearse on. The rug looked very similar to what I would see when I walked onto the TED stage, and it helped me to visualize delivering a world-class speech and presenting confidently. In addition, I also purchased a few new dresses and shoes months ahead of my talk. I would wear the outfits, stand on the red rug, deliver my speech, and visualize every detail of delivering the talk with poise and grace. I imagined being the highest, most confident version of myself and made it come into reality through visualization and action. Every time I would stand on my red circular rug, I would be flooded with gratitude for the opportunity, and it further strengthened my purpose and resolve. If you can visualize yourself doing it and then take the action steps to make that visual as real and tangible as possible, it will build confidence within you that is so strong it will be unshakable with enough time and practice.

Holding Onto Vision in the Face of Change

The only consistent thing in life is change so don't shy away or be afraid of change. Remember, change happens but growth is optional. If you want to truly grow and become highly confident you must be ready to change and to evolve. For you to become your most confident self it is likely that you will need to change your habits, your actions, your thoughts, or your environment so embrace change because change is a catalyst for growth. This is why it is so important to keep your sights set and your vision clear while you are going through your journey. For you to make the necessary changes you need to become confident you need to have such clarity of vision that no matter what you are faced with in life or what changes may come as a result, it won't throw you off course and derail you from achieving your highest, most confident version of yourself.

Practice these positive affirmations to keep your vision-clear and your sights continually set on your goals. Say them as many times as necessary to inspire you to continue with your vision so that it is anchored securely and at the forefront of your mind:

1. I have clarity of vision, and I see the world around me and myself with precision and accuracy.
2. My vision is clear and focused, allowing me to see every detail of my most confident self with ease and accuracy.
3. I trust my intuition to guide me towards clarity and insight in every situation.
4. I am grateful for the gift of clear vision, which allows me to appreciate the beauty of the world around me and within me.
5. My vision is aligned with my purpose and goals, and I take inspired action towards manifesting them through action.

6. I see obstacles as opportunities for growth and development, and I remain focused on my vision of success.
7. I am open to new perspectives and insights that expand my vision and understanding of the world.
8. My vision is guided by my heart and soul, and I trust that everything is unfolding for my highest good.
9. I am in tune with my inner vision, and I trust that it will lead me towards my greatest desires and aspirations.
10. I am grateful for the clarity and insight that comes from a clear vision, and I use it to create a positive impact in the world.

Takeaways from this Chapter:
- *Clarify Your Vision:* Keeping your sights and visualizations of who you want to become clear begins with defining your goals and aspirations with utmost clarity. Be specific about what you want to achieve and visualize yourself embodying your ideal self.
- *Create a Vision Board:* Use visual aids like a vision board to reinforce your aspirations. Compile images,

quotes, and symbols that represent your desired future self. Regularly review your vision board to stay motivated and focused.

- *Cultivate Belief in Your Potential:* Visualizing your ideal self-instills a deep belief in your ability to achieve your goals. When you can see yourself as the person you want to become, it becomes easier to believe that it is possible.

- *Enhance Focus & Direction:* Clear sights and visualizations provide a sense of direction. You are less likely to be swayed by distractions or self-doubt when you have a vivid image of where you want to go and who you want to be.

- *Boost Motivation & Persistence:* Your visions of your ideal self-serve as a constant source of motivation. They inspire you to persist through challenges and setbacks, knowing that the person you aspire to become is within reach.

- *Align Actions with Goals:* Visualizations help you align your daily actions with your long-term goals. Your choices become intentional, as you consistently work towards bringing your vision to life.

- *Overcome Limiting Beliefs:* By repeatedly visualizing your ideal self, you can challenge and overcome limiting beliefs that may hold you back from reaching your full potential.

- *Develop a Positive Mindset:* Visualizations create a positive mindset by focusing on your strengths and aspirations. You cultivate a can-do attitude that propels you forward in your personal growth journey.

Lessons Learned from Keeping Your Sights and Visualizations Clear:

- *The Power of Intention:* Clarity in your sights and visualizations sets a clear intention for your life. This intention acts as a guiding force, directing your decisions and actions towards your desired future.

- *Visualization Enhances Manifestation:* When you consistently visualize your ideal self, you align your thoughts and actions with your goals, making them more likely to manifest.

- *Resilience in the Face of Challenges:* Visualizing your

future self provides a source of strength during tough times. It helps you maintain focus and perseverance, even when obstacles arise.

- *Confidence & Self-Belief:* A clear vision of your ideal self-fosters self-belief and confidence. As you see yourself accomplishing your goals, you strengthen your sense of capability and self-assurance.
- *Living with Purpose:* Keeping your sights and visualizations clear brings purpose and meaning to your life. You have a driving force that inspires you to strive for personal growth and fulfillment.
- *Visualization Creates Positivity:* Regularly engaging in positive visualizations creates a more optimistic outlook on life. You see opportunities where others see challenges and approach life with enthusiasm and hope.
- *A Journey of Self-Discovery:* Your sights and visualizations provide insight into your deepest desires and values. This process becomes a journey of self-discovery, helping you understand yourself on a profound level.

Why It Is Important:

Having clear sights and visualizations of who you want to become is crucial for several reasons. First and foremost, it acts as a powerful motivator, igniting the fire within you to pursue your dreams and aspirations. Clarity in your vision gives you a road map for your journey, providing direction and focus on a world full of distractions.

Furthermore, visualizing your ideal self creates a positive and growth-oriented mindset. It helps you overcome limiting beliefs and empowers you to believe in your potential. As you consistently visualize your goals, you align your thoughts, emotions, and actions with your desired outcomes, making them more achievable.

Ultimately, having clear sights and visualizations of your future self-sets the stage for a fulfilling and purpose-driven life. It is a continuous process that evolves with you, guiding you towards becoming the best version of yourself. Embrace the power of visualization, and watch as it transforms your life, propelling you towards your dreams and aspirations with unwavering determination and confidence.

Your Turn:

1.) What images come to your mind when you think of what success and confidence looks like to you?

2.) What are 10 things that you identify as successful or confident?

3.) What are 10 actions you can perform today to achieve each of these goals?

Chapter 7 Purpose: Where to Start

*In all things, radiate **Purpose**. Be aligned with the reason you are here on this planet and own your purpose with all your will and might. When you are aligned with your purpose there is no competition and there is no room for comparison.*

Before you read this chapter, you may be thinking that the word purpose feels lofty, far-fetched, or out of reach. The topic can be surprisingly divisive as some people may believe that life is by chance and that no one has a defined design specific to them. I understand this because I once felt the same way. There was a period in my life where I questioned if there was a God, a meaning to life, and a greater purpose for each of us. I remember feeling as though I didn't care whether God existed, I didn't believe in a greater calling or an infiniteness of existence. However, it is my goal that after you read this chapter that you have new insights into the word purpose and what it means for your life. I do believe everyone has a purpose and is here for a reason. If your heart is beating, and your lungs are full of air there is a reason you are here on this Earth for which you were specifically created and designed. If you have been traumatized, lived in poverty, or suffered abuse, the topic of purpose may seem fundamentally out of reach for you. However, I assure you that this is not the case but there are steps you must go through to achieve self-actualization and purpose.

In 1943 famed psychologist, Abraham Maslow developed a conceptual framework that illustrates the different levels of human needs and their hierarchical arrangement. The theory suggests that individuals are motivated to fulfill certain fundamental needs, and once those needs are met, they are driven to satisfy higher-level needs. The hierarchy is often represented as a pyramid with five distinct levels, just as this book includes five distinct steps. At the base of the pyramid are the physiological needs, which represent the most fundamental requirements for human survival. These include needs such as food, water, shelter, sleep, and basic bodily functions. These needs must be met first, as they are essential for sustaining life and maintaining overall well-being. Once physiological needs are satisfied, individuals seek safety and security.

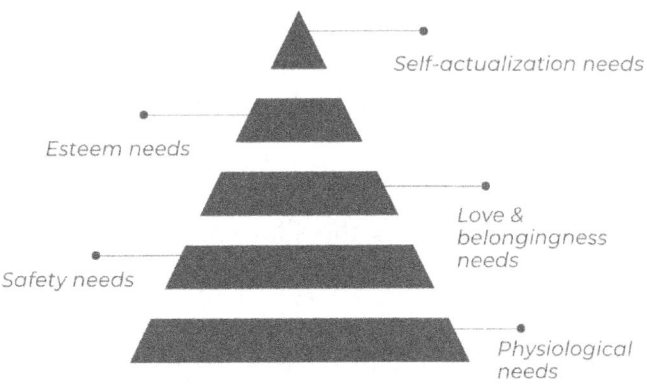

Safety needs encompass the need for physical safety, protection from harm, stability, and a sense of order. This includes factors like personal security, employment security, financial stability, health, and a safe living environment. For many people who suffered from abuse, neglect, poverty, scarcity, or trauma it is difficult to feel safe and as such they are unable to attain higher levels until these needs are met.

When our brains and bodies are conditioned for fight or flight response due to these types of conditions it can be difficult to overcome but certainly not impossible.

Once safety needs are fulfilled, individuals strive for a sense of love, belongingness, and social connection. This includes the need for intimate relationships, friendships, family, and a sense of belonging within a community or social group. Humans are social creatures and desire companionship, affection, and acceptance from others. After the need for love and belongingness are satisfied, individuals seek to develop a positive self-image and gain recognition and respect from others. Esteem needs encompass both internal and external aspects. Internally, it involves developing self-confidence, self-esteem, and a sense of personal accomplishment. Externally, it involves gaining the respect, recognition, and admiration of others through achievements, status, or social validation.

At the top of the pyramid is the concept of self-actualization, which represents the highest level of human needs. Self-actualization involves the realization of one's full potential, personal growth, and the pursuit of self-fulfillment.

It encompasses the desire for creativity, self-expression, knowledge, and the continuous quest for personal growth, meaning, and purpose in life. This is why the concept of confidence and purpose may seem out of reach, especially if you have faced extreme adversity. However, it is attainable once your lower-level needs are met and through practicing the steps outlined in this book and continuous acts of self-care, self-love, and gratitude. Remember that the struggles and hardships you have faced in life were all working toward preparing you for your greater purpose and calling. These lessons do not dictate your future unless you allow them that power. For you to achieve self-actualization and find your purpose it may take time, but it is well worth the journey and effort.

We are all connected, there is no one human who is greater than another, we all have infinite souls created by the same God. The great Erwin Schrödinger once said this beautifully in his famous quote, "the total number of minds in the universe is one." This undoubtedly is one of the most profound statements that has ever been uttered. The singularity that exists that works to bind and unify all things should be enough reason to give you pause and realize exactly how powerful you are and how much purpose you have. When you begin to understand this concept, you realize that the God that created you wants you to live your best life and that it is pleasing to God for you to feel confident and purposeful.

We all belong, have a divine purpose, and have a place. The unfortunate reality is that many people feel purposeless, lost, or broken. They go about life trying to be like other people, they want to blend in, to do what others do and don't realize that they are made to do or be more. The failure to understand that you are a part of a divine plan can lead many people to not realizing their fullest potential in life. They work tirelessly on someone else's dream and spend much of their lives feeling purposeless and lacking confidence. I remember feeling this way. On the surface, it looked like I had a great life but, on the inside, I felt darkness and hopelessness. At my lowest point I didn't want to live anymore. I remember asking my daughter whether she would miss me if I were gone, to realize I needed to hang on.

When you are in a depressed state of mind it can feel

like you are in a dark cave. When you have been in darkness for a long period of time it can be difficult for your eyes to adjust when you enter a brightly lit room. Your eyes may sting when you see light after being in darkness for a period of time but eventually you adjust, and it becomes natural to you again. This is what it is like to come out of a depressive state, you feel surrounded by darkness and light seems unfamiliar to you. However, when you begin to let light, purpose, and God into your life and into your heart there will be no going back. Your purpose becomes so strong that it empowers you to keep pursuing your higher calling and the universe begins to move all things toward you. Confidence and fulfillment become inevitable as you begin to align with your higher calling.

Your Existence Is a Miracle of Nature

As incredible as it sounds, the odds of each one of us being alive is said to be greater than 1 in 400 trillion (400,000,000,000,000). This seemingly incredible calculation is almost unfathomable and is enough to give anyone pause and perspective. All of history has complied and conspired to bring you to life. The nearly undefinable odds that you are reading this book right now are seemingly impossible and it is difficult to wrap our minds around. The odds of each of your ancestors meeting, having children, surviving catastrophes, war, famine, plagues, and natural disasters are so rare that it is almost impossible to imagine and yet here you are, alive, breathing air, with a beating heart in your chest.

The phrase "we are made of star stuff" was famously coined by astronomer Carl Sagan. It refers to the fact that many of the chemical elements that make up our bodies, such as carbon, nitrogen, and oxygen, were forged in the nuclear reactions that occur within stars billions of years ago. When a star reaches the end of its life and explodes in a supernova, it releases all the elements it has produced throughout its lifetime into space. These elements can then go on to form new stars, planets, and even life. As our own solar system was forming, the cloud of gas and dust that would become the Sun and its planets was enriched with these elements from earlier generations of stars. Over time, this material coalesced to form the planets, including Earth, and the organic molecules that eventually gave rise to life. Every atom of oxygen in our lungs, the carbon in our bodies, the calcium in our bones and the iron in our blood was created inside a star before Earth was formed. So, in a very real sense, we truly are made of star stuff and each one of us is a living, breathing, miracle of nature. Within each of us resides great power and potential, the very universe resides within us along with its capacity for growth and expansion. Through this understanding we can also infer that each one of us, regardless of our background or what we have gone through all have equal potential. There is nothing less about you than anyone else, you have the potential of the universe inside every atom and within every cell of your body.

Anytime I start feeling unconfident or unsure of myself I am reminded of the incredibly powerfully odds of me being alive and it works to set me back on track. Don't ever forget what you are made of and how much power and potential that exists within you. When we realize just how rare and precious life is, it can be incredibly uplifting and empowering. It can remind us to live each day to the fullest, to appreciate the little moments of joy and wonder that surround us, and to make the most of the time we have. It can inspire us to be kind, compassionate, and loving towards others, recognizing that every life is just as precious as our own. Every day, we are surrounded by countless examples of the beauty and wonder of life. From the intricate patterns of a butterfly's wings to the vast expanse of the night sky, there is so much to appreciate and marvel at. Perhaps most importantly, we can form deep connections with other living beings, to love and be loved, to share our experiences and make a difference in the world. So, let's cherish this gift of life that we've been given, and make the most of every moment. Let's live with purpose and passion, savoring every experience and striving to make a positive impact on the world. And let's never forget just how rare and precious this gift truly is.

From the Human Cell to the Universe, Everything Points to an Interconnected Purpose

Each cell in our body has a unique purpose and so do each of us as individuals. I often use this as an analogy with clients and audience members I speak to, and it tends to resonate with them deeply about purpose. If we look at the human body, we see that each individual cell has a particular function. Heart cells, lung cells, skin cells, eye cells, neurological cells, blood cells, etc., all have specific functionality and defined purpose. So, what would happen if a blood cell decided it wanted to be a heart cell or a skin cell? It is likely that that heart cell would fail in its new role as it is not equipped for the function it is called on to perform and the cell would go the rest of its life feeling inadequate, inept, and like a failure. There is nothing wrong with this cell and its functionality if it is living to its specifically designed purpose. The longer the cell continues in the wrong path, the longer it will not live up to its goals or purpose.

Similarly, each of us has our own unique talents, skills, and passions that give us a sense of purpose and direction in life. Just as each cell in our body contributes to the overall functioning of our body, each of us contributes to the world around us in our own unique way. Whether it's through our work, our relationships, or our creative pursuits, we all have something to offer that helps make the world a better place. The uniqueness of each individual cell in our body also reflects the diversity of life itself. Each person is different, with their own unique experiences, perspectives, and identities. Our differences are what make us interesting and valuable, and they provide us with the opportunity to learn from one another and to create a more inclusive and compassionate world. Just as our cells work together to create a healthy, functioning body, we must work together to create a healthy, functioning society. Our cells do not compete but rather they collaborate and work together to achieve a greater purpose which is to keep you alive and healthy. Each of us has a role to play in creating a world that is more just, equitable, and sustainable. By embracing our uniqueness and working together towards a common goal, we can create a better future for ourselves and for generations to come.

<u>Competition only exists when you are doing something for which you are not specifically designed.</u> When each cell of your body aligns with their unique design, there is no competition, there is only collaboration and as a result, the entire body benefits, and functions more optimally. The cells in our body work together in a highly coordinated

and complex manner, with each cell playing a unique role in maintaining the overall health and function of the body. Cells also collaborate through the formation of tissues and organs. Different types of cells come together to form tissues such as muscle, bone, and skin, which in turn combine to form organs such as the heart, lungs, and liver. Within these tissues and organs, cells work together to carry out specialized functions, such as contracting to move the body, filtering waste from the blood, or producing hormones that regulate metabolism. Overall, the collaboration and coordination of cells is essential for maintaining the health and function of the body. By working together, cells can carry out a wide range of activities and respond to changing conditions, helping to ensure that the body can adapt and thrive in a constantly changing environment. Your body is beautifully designed and is working diligently and collectively to keep you alive. Have gratitude for the work it is doing so that you can accomplish your greater purpose.

Imagine if the cells in our bodies didn't collaborate and instead worked against each other. This internal competition would lead to a breakdown in the overall function of the body, which could have serious health consequences. For example, immune cells might start attacking healthy cells in the body, leading to autoimmune disorders such as rheumatoid arthritis or multiple sclerosis. Similarly, cancer can occur when cells start dividing and growing uncontrollably, without regard for the needs of the surrounding tissue. If cells didn't collaborate, the body might also struggle to respond effectively to stress or injury. For example, after an injury, cells need to work together to repair the damaged tissue and reduce inflammation. Without collaboration, this process might be impaired, leading to chronic pain or impaired healing. Overall, the collaboration of cells is essential for the overall health and function of the body. Without collaboration, the body would be more vulnerable to disease and injury and would struggle to adapt and respond to changing conditions. So, it's clear that the ability of cells to work together and coordinate their activities is essential for the proper functioning of our bodies, and for maintaining our overall health and wellbeing.

You are a vessel of possibilities, and a manifestation of intelligent design. Your body is an intricately woven masterpiece, a testament to the wonders of creation. It has been granted the ability to think, to feel, to love, and to make a difference in the world. How can you not feel purposeful when you realize that every breath you take, every beat of your heart, is a testament to the incredible journey that lies before you?

Embrace the awe-inspiring truth that your existence is not a mere accident, but a deliberate creation. You are here for a reason, with a unique combination of talents, passions, and experiences. Your intelligently designed body serves as a vessel for the expression of your purpose in this world. Just as your cells were not designed to compete, we are not designed to compete. We are social beings who were designed to collaborate and support each other and our unique purposes. Competition leads to fear and scarcity and decreases creativity. Highly confident people are creative collaborators, they do not suffer insecurity from someone else's greatness or potential. Highly confident people can recognize their own greatness and potential and view others as complements to them, not threats. By working with others, we can leverage diverse perspectives, skills, and experiences to come up with innovative solutions to complex problems. We can learn from one another, build upon each other's strengths, and support each other through challenges and setbacks. Moreover, collaboration has the power to foster a sense of community and belonging, as individuals come together around shared values and goals.

When we collaborate, we can create a sense of shared ownership and investment in the outcomes we are working towards, which can create a sense of fulfillment and purpose that goes beyond individual success. Ultimately, collaboration is about recognizing the potential for greatness that lies within each of us and working together to bring that greatness to life. It's about recognizing that we are all interconnected, and that we all have a role to play in creating a better world for ourselves and for future generations. So, if you want to create lasting change and make a real impact in the world, start by embracing collaboration. Reach out to others, listen to their ideas and perspectives, and work together towards a shared vision of a brighter future. With collaboration, anything is possible, including your ability to build confidence within yourself. Instead of competing with anyone, collaboration allows you to grow in your confidence because you begin to see how valuable you are to someone else and understand your unique skillsets and abilities with more depth of clarity.

First Steps Toward Your Purpose

Finding one's life purpose is a personal and complex journey that may take time, reflection, and exploration. Your purpose may change and evolve over time. You may lose sight of it for a period and must rediscover the meaning in your life, this is perfectly normal and apart of the growth process. Whether you are trying to rediscover a sense of purpose or find your purpose for the first time, there are practical steps you can take to begin your journey.

- Take time to reflect on what's most important to you and what activities, hobbies, or interests bring you joy and fulfillment. What are the things that make you feel excited, engaged, and alive?
- Consider the skills and talents you possess and how

you could use them to make a positive impact on the world. What are the things you do well, and what do people often come to you for help with?

- Experiment with different activities or pursuits that align with your values, passions, and skills. Attend workshops, volunteer in different organizations, or take up a new hobby to discover what resonates with you.
- Think about the moments in your life when you felt most fulfilled or experienced a sense of purpose. What was it about those experiences that made you feel that way?
- Talk to friends, family, or a professional coach or mentor who can help you navigate the journey of discovering your life purpose.

Don't overthink it. Your purpose is a part of you, and it is why you were specifically designed and created. For some, your purpose is that little thing in the back of your mind that has always been there but maybe you have resisted it for one reason or another. Perhaps someone told you that the thing you are purposeful or passionate about was not a viable career choice or that you couldn't make money doing it, so you stopped pursuing it. Perhaps you wanted to be responsible but no matter what, you couldn't stop thinking about it. As you continue in your journey of becoming your most confident and purposeful self, remember to challenge the limiting beliefs of others. Someone may have told you that your purpose and passions were not a smart move for you to make and that it would result in failure if you were to go after them. If one person has made a living doing what you want to do than it is possible for you to do so as well. The only limitation is in our minds and through the amount of action we take. If you believe it, can visualize yourself doing it, if it makes you feel alive, if it contributes to the betterment of all, and if you can make a living doing it then don't let anyone stop you, including yourself.

Finding Your Ikigai

The term "ikigai" is a Japanese concept that refers to a person's reason for being or their sense of purpose in life. It is a philosophy that emphasizes finding joy, fulfillment, and a sense of meaning or purpose in one's existence. Ikigai helps individuals identify and connect with their sense of purpose, providing a deeper meaning to their lives. Having a clear purpose gives people a reason to wake up in the morning and motivates them to pursue their goals and aspirations. By understanding their passions, skills, and the needs of the world, individuals can align their actions and decisions with their core values. This alignment leads to a greater sense of authenticity and satisfaction in life. Ikigai encourages individuals to explore the intersections of different aspects of life, such as work, hobbies, relationships, and personal growth. It emphasizes that a balanced and harmonious integration of these domains leads to a more fulfilling and well-rounded life. Finding and pursuing one's ikigai is associated with improved psychological well-being. Engaging in activities that one loves and excels at, while making a positive impact on the world, promotes feelings of joy, accomplishment, and self-worth. Ikigai provides individuals with a source of resilience during challenging times. When faced with obstacles or setbacks, a clear sense of purpose and passion can fuel motivation, perseverance, and the ability to overcome difficulties.

Allow yourself to explore your talents, strengths, natural gifts, passions, and skillsets. Simply reflect on what you are passionate about and interested in and follow the below questions for guidance.

- **What you love:** This refers to your passions, interests, and activities that bring you joy and fulfillment.

  Your Turn: What do you love, what brings you joy?

- **What you are good at:** This represents your skills, talents, and abilities. It encompasses the things you excel at or have expertise in.

  Your Turn: What are you an expert at, what is easy and natural for you?

- **What the world needs:** This involves identifying the needs and problems of the world around you. It focuses on the ways in which you can contribute and make a positive impact.

  Your Turn: Does this solve a problem for people and their lives better?

- **What you can be paid for:** This refers to the practical aspect of sustaining yourself financially. It involves finding opportunities where your skills and passions align with market demand.

  Your Turn: Do you feel a mental block with money, and do you find it difficult to ask for what you deserve?

Remember that there is no shame in making money and being financially stable. For you to accomplish your purpose you will need to live a full life and part of that requires you to make money. This can be a difficult concept for many people to understand, especially if they grew up surrounded by scarcity, lack, and poverty as I did. However, money is an essential aspect of life and to live fully and help others, you need to be able to produce income for yourself. You will find that when you align with your purpose you will attract others who need the exact service or remedy that you offer, you will be seen as a specialist to them and as such you will be in great demand. Your purpose opens the doors for success but for you to live fully in your purpose, scarce thinking about money will need to be shifted. Once this shift takes place, it leads to unstoppable confidence and a sense of self-belief that is nearly indescribable.

When I first began my entrepreneurship journey, I recall needing to challenge my scarcity mindset surrounding money. I simply wasn't charging enough and as a result I wasn't attracting aligned clients. I couldn't understand why clients wouldn't want to work with me until I realized how unconfident I was at presenting my offer and how my mindset about money was blocking my success. It wasn't that I was unworthy or undeserving, it was that I wasn't asking for what I was worth. Ultimately until I realized my worth, I would not become successful and confident as a business owner. I started by becoming aware of my beliefs surrounding money and any blocks or limitations I had. My upbringing and personal experiences shaped many of my views on money and I began to recognize the negative or limiting beliefs I was holding onto. I realized that money, just like confidence is not for other people as I once thought, money is also not scarce or evil. I worked to challenge these limiting beliefs and blockages that were holding me back. I realized that money was essential for me to live a truly fulfilling life and once I became confident and abundant in thinking and self-belief, clients became more and more abundant as well.

Focus On Your Strengths

For years, I took any skills or talents that I had, and I dismissed them and would tell myself that there was someone out there who was better, more talented, had more recourses or was smarter. I convinced myself that there was no point in pursuing something I loved because it wouldn't pay the bills and that there was no time for passion projects. However, when I began working on my business full-time, I realized that those false narratives could not have been any further from the truth. I was a problem-solver, and I had a certain skillset that other people did not have. I started to pay attention to things that I liked and things I was naturally talented at. I began noticing people's reactions after I helped them with something that they were not proficient at, and I started to see a pattern. Focusing on my strengths enabled me to build massive amounts of confidence.

When you focus on what you're good at, you're more likely to feel competent, capable, and successful. This, in turn, helps to boost your self-esteem and confidence. One of the reasons why focusing on your strengths can be so effective is because it helps you to develop a sense of mastery. When you're doing something that you're good at, you're more likely to feel in control and able to accomplish your goals. When you are doing something that comes naturally to you, you are more likely to enjoy it, which in turn makes it easier to stay focused and committed to the task at hand. This feeling of mastery can help to counteract feelings of helplessness or inadequacy that can undermine your confidence. Moreover, focusing on your strengths can also help you to develop a more positive self-image. When you recognize your strengths and acknowledge your accomplishments, you're more likely to see yourself as a capable and worthy individual. This positive self-image can help to counteract negative self-talk and doubts that can erode your confidence.

Focusing on your strengths can also help you to set and achieve meaningful goals. When you're clear about what you're good at and what you want to accomplish, you're more likely to make progress and feel a sense of accomplishment. This can be especially important when you're facing challenges or setbacks, as it can help to keep you motivated and focused on your goals. When we focus on our strengths, we can identify areas where we can continue to grow and develop. We can use our strengths as a foundation to build upon, and work to develop new skills and abilities that complement and enhance our existing strengths. This process of continual learning and growth can lead to mastery over time, as we become more and more skilled and proficient in our chosen field.

Turning Fear or Pain into Purpose

For me personally, finding my purpose was a journey and it did not happen overnight. If you are someone who has been abused, traumatized, or lived in poverty, it can seem difficult to find your purpose, but it is not impossible. I remember saying to myself that I would never be able to raise my voice or speak publicly, it was my biggest fear.

Sometimes the things you are the most afraid of are a part of your purpose, we may be fearful of them because of limiting beliefs, lack of confidence, or imposter syndrome but if something excites you and ignites curiosity within you, it is worth exploring on a deeper level. Growing up feeling as though I didn't have a voice and being terrified of speaking publicly kept me at bay for many years of my life. However, slowly but surely and with enough self-work and self-belief, I began to understand that my fear was not actually speaking but a fear of rejection and it terrified me to imagine what people thought of me. These fears prevented my growth and for years I remained bound and tied by them as a result.

I came to the revelation that I would not be able to help as many people as I needed to if I didn't overcome my fears, limiting beliefs, self-doubt, and lack of confidence once and for all. If I didn't face my fears, I would be doomed to stagnation and I began to fear stagnation more than I feared the unknown. You become an unstoppable force once your fear of staying the same outweighs your fear of failure, rejection, and ridicule. I knew that for me to become truly confident I needed to face my biggest fear which had been present my entire life, public speaking.

One evening while my family and I were at dinner I received an unexpected call from my friend who is a professional speaker. He told me that he would be speaking at a conference in three days and that one of the keynote speakers had injured his back and as a result would be unable to make the event. He asked me if I would be willing to deliver a keynote on such short notice. While I was terrified, I said yes because I knew this would be a major opportunity to face my fear and prove to myself that I could do it. Prior to delivering my speech I faced several obstacles. For starters, I was given very short notice and it was all the way in Washington, D.C which is about five hours from my home. Between client meetings and appointments that week, I only had about twenty minutes to prepare my keynote. On top of this, my glasses broke the day prior, and I had to super glue them together to make the drive to Washington. However, something told me to act on the opportunity and seize the moment. After all, where there is a will, there is a way, and I was determined to face my fears head on.

I prepared my speech to the best of my ability and practiced once in the bathroom mirror prior to making the drive. I decided that my talk would be impactful and started visualizing a strong delivery that led to a standing ovation at the end. I wanted to go big with my delivery and leave a lasting impression with the audience, I was determined to create lasting and life-changing impact. I decided to tell a small fraction of my story in the last slide of my presentation and told the audience why I was there that day. I told the audience the reason I was there that day delivering my speech was due to my ability to network and form deep and meaningful professional relationships but also because only eight months earlier I chose life and decided against the act of suicide.

You could have heard a pen drop when I said those words. No one except for the person who invited me knew this part of my story. By sharing my story, showing vulnerability and authenticity, I found myself further aligning with my purpose and it helped me to realize that the pain of my past can be utilized to create a powerful connection with other people. As an author, speaker, and leader, I need to be authentic because readers are looking for a genuine connection to me and to my story. Readers and audience members want to feel like they are being let into my world and experiencing something real and relatable. Authenticity allows someone to connect with you on a deeper level and to trust that the story being told is honest and true. Through authenticity, and by tapping into your own unique experiences and perspectives can help to create a more compelling and engaging story. By being true to yourself and your own voice, you can create stories that resonate and leave a lasting impact.

As I began to walk off stage, I began to hear applause and then I took note as people began to stand up. The person who was managing the event rushed to the stage to tell me to get back up. I whispered to him that this was my first time on stage, and he couldn't believe it, then he announced it to the room that this was my first speech. The crowd responded with sounds of shock and surprise.

As I made my way through the crowd, shaking hands, exchanging business cards and networking, no one could believe that that was my first time delivering a speech publicly. I received so many compliments, I truly didn't know what to do with myself. I was on top of the world and finally felt like a super confident person. I was aligned with my purpose finally and there was no stopping me.

It turns out, public speaking is as natural to me as drinking water or breathing air, it takes little effort for me, and I feel like my most confident version of myself when I am on stage. What was once my biggest fear is now something that excites me and makes me feel alive. As someone who is naturally reserved, it was challenging for me to share my story at first. Afterall, I was in a room full of unfamiliar faces, but I realized that for me to create human connection, I needed to share.

Sharing your story with the world can be a powerful and cathartic experience, but it's important to do so mindfully. If you feel that sharing your story contributes to your purpose, try using this framework before sharing, to achieve the outcome you desire.

- **Consider your motivation for sharing.** Are you seeking validation, understanding, or hoping to help others? It's important to be honest with yourself about your intentions and ensure that you're not using your story to seek attention or pity.
- **Think about your audience.** Who are you sharing your story with, and why? Are you speaking to close friends and family, or are you sharing your story publicly? It's important to consider your audience's emotional capacity and ensure that you're not causing them unnecessary distress. Be mindful of potential

triggers and sensitive topics and approach your storytelling with compassion and empathy.

- **Set boundaries** and only share what you're comfortable with. You don't owe anyone the full details of your experiences, and it's okay to withhold certain information if it feels too personal or private. Additionally, consider the potential impact of your story on your personal and professional life. While vulnerability and authenticity can be powerful, it's important to protect your privacy and avoid sharing anything that could negatively impact your well-being.

Remember that sharing your story is a process, and it's okay to take things slowly. You don't have to share everything at once, and it's important to prioritize your own emotional needs throughout the process. Be patient with yourself, and seek support from trusted friends, family members, or mental health professionals as needed. By approaching your storytelling with mindfulness and intentionality, you can share your story with the world in a way that is both authentic and respectful.

Speaking can be a powerful way to build confidence. When you speak up and express yourself, you're taking a risk and putting yourself out there. This can be challenging, especially if you're not used to speaking up or if you're worried about what others might think of you. However, by practicing speaking and developing your skills, you can build your confidence and feel more comfortable expressing yourself.

One of the main ways that speaking can build confidence is by helping you to develop your communication skills. When you're able to communicate effectively, you're more likely to feel confident in your ability to express yourself and make yourself understood. This can be especially important in professional settings, where effective communication is often key to success. Speaking can also help you to develop your self-awareness and self-expression. When you take the time to reflect on your thoughts and feelings, and then express them to others, you're developing a stronger sense of who you are and what you stand for. This can be an important aspect of building confidence, as it can help you to feel more grounded and authentic in your interactions with others. Speaking can also help you to overcome fear and anxiety. When you face your fears and speak up despite feeling nervous or uncertain, you're developing resilience and courage. Over time, this can help you to feel more confident in your ability to handle challenging situations and to trust in yourself.

Don't be afraid to move forward with something that scares you, the things that scare you the most may just be a part of your purpose and pursing them could give you great power. For me, I became more fearful of being the same person next year and I was tired of living my life the same year after year. It was time for a change, and I was ready to do anything to move me forward. For the first time in my life, I wasn't controlled by fear, I felt confident and felt invincible. When you begin to trust your deepest truths and find your purpose, a more confident version of you begins to emerge and you metamorphosize into your highest version of yourself. You sprout wings like a butterfly and other people start to take notice. Purpose attracts purpose and purposeful people begin to be attracted to you as a result.

Trade Anxiety for Purpose

In Easter of 2022, shortly after I had quit my toxic corporate job, my family and I decided to go on a beach trip and get away for a bit. I didn't have a steady source of income, but I knew getting away would be good for all of us. Every vacation I had been on until this point was planned, and every exhausting detail was thought of. I made sure that we knew what restaurants we were eating at, what times we needed to be places and exactly where we were going. I made lists or spreadsheets for vacations which is about as fun as it sounds. My mind was continually living in the future, and the present moments were the last thing on my mind, until this vacation.

We decided to travel to the Outer Banks, which is an amazing city on the Atlantic coast in North Carolina. It's about a 4.5-hour drive from our home, so while it is drivable in a day, it takes a considerable amount of time to get there. The old me would have spent the drive planning exhaustively, imagining every possible scenario, and have every detail covered with plans in place for every eventuality. But something was beginning to change deep within me.

When we arrived that day, and my husband turned to me to ask where we were eating for lunch, I looked at him dumbfounded and said, "I have no idea."

I honestly hadn't thought about it for a second which was completely uncharacteristic of me. I ended up looking up options and picked the third thing I saw and settled on it. The old me would have exhausted my efforts browsing and scouring looking for the perfect option but that person was slowly dissipating.

Overplanning can be a symptom of anxiety because it can stem from a need for control and a fear of uncertainty. People with anxiety often experience a heightened sense of worry and fear, which can lead them to try to control every aspect of their lives to minimize the potential for negative outcomes. In the case of overplanning, this can manifest as an excessive focus on details and a need to plan and prepare for every possible scenario. While some planning can be helpful in achieving goals and reducing stress, overplanning can become a form of avoidance or procrastination, as individuals may become so focused on planning that they are unable to act or move forward with their goals. Overplanning can also lead to a cycle of self-doubt and second-guessing, as individuals may feel like they are never fully prepared or that there are always more things to plan for. This can lead to feelings of anxiety, stress, and overwhelm, which can ultimately make it harder to act and achieve goals.

To break the cycle of overplanning and anxiety, it can be helpful to practice mindfulness and focus on the present moment. Rather than constantly worrying about the future, try to stay grounded in the present and focus on what you can control in the moment. This can help you feel calmer and centered and can reduce your overall levels of anxiety. It can also be helpful to challenge your thoughts and beliefs about planning and control. Ask yourself if your need for control is truly serving you, or if it is causing more harm than good. Consider experimenting with letting go of some of your plans and allowing things to unfold naturally. You may be surprised at how freeing it can feel to let go of control and trust in the universe.

After lunch we decided to hit the beach. Our hotel was not available for a few hours, so we changed into our bathing suits in the restaurant restroom and went to the beach and hang out. My daughter was six years old at the time and is a total beach girl in every sense of the word. She loves the beach, and it is her favorite place on Earth. I remember her sprinting towards the crashing waves and seeing her face light up as the cold ocean water hit her feet. She was laughing hysterically at the ocean as she ran up and down the surf. Seeing her excitement sparked something in me and I ran towards her to experience what she was experiencing. At that moment I chose joy. I began to laugh out loud with her as we kept getting splashed by cold ocean water and at that moment, I experienced true joy for the first time in years. I felt like a kid again and I couldn't believe how much of my life I went without joy once I felt it.

I want to emphasize the word "choose" in reference to joy. At any point in time, regardless of the situation we are facing, we can choose joy and have gratitude, but to fully experience feelings of joy and gratitude you need to be present minded. Through a present mind, you can better explore and understand your interests, desires, and unique talents. By being fully engaged in the present, you can more readily recognize the opportunities, experiences, and connections that align with your authentic self. This awareness and alignment help guide you towards discovering your purpose and what brings you joy, fulfillment, and a sense of meaning in your life.

A present mind allows you to engage fully in the present moment, making conscious choices, and taking intentional actions that align with your values and purpose. It helps you navigate through life with greater clarity, authenticity, and a sense of direction, leading you towards a path that resonates with your deepest sense of purpose and fulfillment.

When you align with your purpose, the activity you are performing can be as natural to you as breathing, drinking water or walking. Start paying attention to things that come naturally to you, get you excited, and make you feel joyful. These things could very well be a part of your purpose and why you were put on this planet, but it is important to note that they could be something you are afraid of or outside your comfort zone. Remember, growth, purpose, and impact exist outside your comfort zone, not within it. For you to live a truly purposeful life and create the impact you desire you need to become a person who is not guided by fear, only purpose.

Sometimes our purpose is that thing we have been resisting or something that we are avoiding but it keeps resurfacing because it is something we were meant to do. However, you must fail, you must learn, and you need to be patient. Purpose sometimes requires resistance, hardship, or time to refine. Through my experience I have found that the greater the adversity that is presented to an individual, the greater the intensity of their purpose. Do not look back in regret or remorse of your past, instead view every failure and trial with the mindset that it has been setting you up to be the person you were meant to become so that you could serve humanity with adequacy. Your pain, your past, your failures, and your trauma have all been a part of what you need to accomplish your purpose and why you are here, be grateful for the journey.

Remember, you are the only person that has ever lived who has your exact perspective on life. Sharing your story can very well be a part of your purpose, just as it is for me. If I wouldn't have shared my story, I would not have become a TEDx speaker or author; and once I aligned with my purpose, my life completely transformed. My purpose is to change lives through my story and help as many people as I can live their fullest, most successful, and purposeful lives by developing confidence. Your purpose will not only serve you but also lead to the betterment of humanity.

Takeaways from this Chapter:

- *Reflect on Your Passions:* Finding your purpose begins with reflecting on your passions and interests. What activities make you lose track of time? Exploring your passions can lead you to your life's purpose.
- *Listen to Your Intuition:* Pay attention to your inner voice and intuition. Often, your instincts will guide you towards opportunities and experiences aligned with your purpose.
- *Seek Meaning & Impact:* Purpose is often connected to making a meaningful impact on others or the world. Look for ways your skills and passions can contribute to the greater good.
- *Be Open to Exploration:* Don't be afraid to explore

various paths. Finding your purpose might involve trying new things and learning from experiences that shape your journey.

- *Seek Guidance & Support:* Seek guidance from mentors, coaches, or spiritual guides who can help you gain clarity on your purpose. Engaging with like-minded individuals can provide valuable insights and support.
- *Stay Persistent:* Discovering your purpose can be a lifelong journey. Stay persistent, and trust that your path will unfold in due time. Embrace every step of the process, even if it takes time to find your true calling.

Lessons Learned from Finding Your Purpose:

- *Fulfillment & Contentment:* Living a purpose-driven life brings deep fulfillment and contentment. When you know your purpose, every day becomes a meaningful and rewarding experience.
- *A Sense of Direction:* Discovering your purpose provides a clear sense of direction in life. You have a

compelling reason to wake up each day and pursue your goals with passion and enthusiasm.

- *Overcoming Challenges:* Knowing your purpose gives you the strength to overcome challenges and persevere during difficult times. Your sense of purpose acts as a guiding light through the darkest moments.
- *Connection & Unity:* Recognizing that we all have a specific purpose fosters a sense of connection and unity with others. Regardless of our diverse backgrounds, we share a common purpose – to make a positive impact on the world.
- *Transcending Circumstances:* Finding your purpose reminds you that your past or current circumstances don't define you. No matter where you were born or what you have been through, you have a unique purpose and reason for being alive.
- *Unleashing Potential:* Embracing your purpose unleashes your full potential. You tap into your inherent talents and abilities, reaching heights you may never have imagined.
- *A Life of Meaning:* Discovering your purpose allows

you to live a life of deep meaning and significance. You become a beacon of inspiration, motivating others to find their purpose and embrace their unique paths.

Why It Is Important:

Recognizing that we all have a specific purpose for which we were designed is of profound importance. It reminds us that we are not merely passive observers in life but active participants with a meaningful role to play.

Regardless of where we were born or the challenges we faced; our purpose transcends circumstances. It acts as a beacon of hope, guiding us through the darkest times and empowering us to rise above adversity.

Knowing your purpose infuses every aspect of your life with a deeper sense of meaning and fulfillment. It aligns your actions with your authentic self, leading to a life of purpose and impact.

Remember, discovering your purpose is a journey unique to everyone. Embrace the process with curiosity, courage, and openness, for your purpose is waiting to be unveiled, illuminating the path to your most purposeful and meaningful life.

Your Turn:

1.) What is something that you are uncomfortable with, but you know would benefit you by doing it (ex: public speaking)?

2.) What steps are you willing to take today to get outside of your comfort zone?

3.) List 10 strengths (brag about yourself):

Chapter 8 – Purpose: Identifying Your Core Values

Unveiling your purpose starts with uncovering your core values—the guiding compass that illuminates your path, fuels your passions, and ignites a life of genuine meaning. Discover why identifying these foundational principles is the pivotal step towards unlocking your true purpose and unleashing a life of extraordinary fulfillment. Core values can help you identify what you are passionate about and guide you to your greater purpose. Core values should be a driving force in your life. They guide your path and help steer your ship, even in foggy weather and during storms.

When I was working in my corporate career, I couldn't figure out why I was struggling, I kept thinking I just needed one more of something (degree, certification, or accolade) to get where I wanted to be in life. I saw people who were less qualified, less educated, less talented, or not as knowledgeable as I was making more money and achieving greater success than I was able to. Of course, to some degree this reflected my level of confidence, which at that time was about as close to zero as you could get, but it also had to do with something else.

My entire life up until this point was spent living someone else's dream and version of success. Like many people I thought if I just climbed the ladder of success and kept pushing, I would finally be able to remove myself from my upbringing and rise above any conditions I was raised in. This was not the case. I kept disappointing myself routinely and failing. Before I could begin to even think about such a thing as a purpose, which at the time seemed far-fetched, I had to attain an understanding of what I wanted, what I believed in, and why I believed in it. This is commonly referred to as your "why" by many people, but it is more involved and deeper than most people understand it to be. Most clients that I have worked with tend to view their "why" as their children, their spouse, or something else external to themselves, but I believe that your "why" starts within you. While it can be shaped and impacted by experiences, people, and other events it is something that exists deep within your soul, and it is the gateway into understanding who you are and what your purpose is. When I achieved clarity on my core values and started getting granular about what I believed in, my purpose, my "why," everything unfurled before my eyes. It was as if a map was laid out before me that directed my next move and the choices, I needed to make to get me to my goals and help me become confident.

As you continue your journey of self-discovery, self-awareness, and confidence-building, you may face times and situations that test your core values but never let them get you off track permanently. Always remember and reflect on your why and keep pushing onward. In times of doubt or uncertainty, reflect on this poem from the great Mother Teresa. Remember that we can never control what other people will do or how they will react, but we always have control of what we do and how we act. Make the conscious choice to act intentionally and with your core values and principles in mind.

"People are often unreasonable, illogical and self-centered;

Forgive them anyway.

If you are kind, people may accuse you of selfish, ulterior motives;

Be kind anyway.

If you are successful, you will win some false friends and some true enemies;

Succeed anyway.

If you are honest and frank, people may cheat you;

Be honest and frank anyway.

What you spend years building, someone could destroy overnight;

Build anyway.

If you find serenity and happiness, they may be jealous;

Be happy anyway.

The good you do today, people will often forget tomorrow;

Do good anyway.

Give the world the best you have, and it may never be enough;

Give the world the best you've got anyway.

You see, in the final analysis, it is between you and your God; It was never between you and them anyway."

-Mother Teresa

Core values are fundamental beliefs or principles that guide behavior. While many people associate core values with companies, individuals can also benefit from identifying and living by their own core values. Here are some of the areas in which I have found core values to be useful:

- **Clarity and Direction:** By identifying what values are most important to you, you can better understand your own priorities and what you want to achieve in life.

- **Decision-Making:** When faced with a difficult choice, you can turn to your core values to guide you towards the decision that aligns with your values.

- **Authenticity:** By staying true to your values, you can avoid compromising yourself or your beliefs for the sake of others.

- **Relationships:** Both personal and professional. When you share values with others, it can help build stronger connections and foster trust.

You may be wondering what this has to do with building your confidence, but it has more to do than confidence that you may realize because this is all working on building the foundation and structure of who you are and ultimately the best version of yourself. Through taking a deep and uncovered understanding of who I was and what I believed in that I finally started to feel confident and purposeful.

It is common to think of core values as outward displays for others, but they can also be applied inwardly to ourselves. When you live and breathe your core values it means that you follow them with every deed you perform, in the way you think, speak, and act towards others and yourself. I showed myself that I valued freedom by quitting my toxic workplace once and for all and being brave enough to do it on my own, I also knew that I would never be subjected to being put in a box ever again by anyone. This seemingly simple exercise of identifying my top core values may not have seemed incredibly impactful at the time, but by having well-defined core values it helped pave the way of self-understanding on a soul level.

Identifying your top 3-5 core values can be a challenging but rewarding process that can help guide present and future decision making. Spend some time reflecting on what matters most to you in life. Think about what brings you the most joy and fulfillment, and what values you admire in others. Make a list of values that resonate with you. Some examples might include honesty, kindness, perseverance, creativity, fairness, or generosity. Try to come up with as many values as possible, without limiting yourself.

If you are having a mental block, take a break from your daily routine and explore a new environment. Try taking a walk-in nature, sit quietly in reflection, and meditate, or go somewhere that inspires you. If you still feel stuck, try out different hobbies and activities but don't be afraid to step outside of your comfort zone and try something new. Sometimes a good way to start is also by taking a personality test to better understand yourself and your values with more clarity. If you haven't identified your core values yet this may take some time and soul-searching but eventually, they will begin to speak to you. Concentrate on what you want out of life, what gives you energy, what motivates you or what excites you and what you believe in profoundly without reservation.

Once you have a list of potential values, start to narrow

it down to your top 10. You can do this by considering which values you feel the most strongly about, and which ones you couldn't live without. Once you have your top 10 values, rank them in order of importance. You can do this by considering which values you prioritize the most, and which ones you are willing to sacrifice. Finally, refine your list down to your top 5 core values. Write them down. Simply saying them out loud is not enough, make them real and tangible by writing them down and put pen to paper. These should be the values that you feel most strongly about, and that you want to guide your decisions and actions in life. By identifying your core values, you can live a more purpose-driven life and make decisions that align with your goals and what you truly believe in.

Clearly defining my core values helped me to lay a path and establish a foundation that I could live by. It helped guide every movement, every action, every decision, and made my choices crystal clear. I decided I no longer wanted to live a life I wanted to escape from, by having conviction in my core values and beliefs it made it easier to not want to escape and for the first time in my life, I felt like I was running towards something instead of away from it.

My Top Core Values:

- Love
- Kindness
- Faith
- Impact
- Freedom

Love

As I held my daughter's hand that day on the beach at the Outer Banks, I felt an energy and I paid attention to it. That energy was love. I felt it leaving my body and going into hers and then I felt her love energy going into mine. It was warm, pure, and there was profound truth in the experience. This is love in its purest form, it is inviting and exciting, but it also heals and magnifies any amount of existing love you have in your body.

Many religious and spiritual traditions believe that God is love and that love is a fundamental aspect of the universe. From this perspective, it is believed that love exists everywhere and is within everything, as it is an essential aspect of the divine. Some spiritual traditions see the universe as an interconnected web of energy, where everything is unified and part of a larger whole. In this view, love is seen as the force that holds everything together and connects us all. Other spiritual traditions view love as a divine spark within everyone, that is waiting to be awakened and expressed. This view suggests that love is not just something that exists externally but is also something that we can cultivate within ourselves through spiritual practices such as meditation, prayer, and acts of service. Regardless of the specific spiritual tradition or belief system, the idea that God is love and that love exists everywhere and within everything is a powerful and uplifting concept. It reminds us that we are all connected and that we are all part of something larger than ourselves. It also encourages us to cultivate love and compassion in our own lives, to connect more deeply with the divine and with each other.

Love is the most powerful force in the universe. Love binds all things, is within all things, and through love all things become possible. Love is responsible for the creation of everything that exists around you. From the distant planets of our universe to the interspaces which unify all things, love exists. Through the power of love, your life became possible and because of its enormous power and potential, you were brought into existence. Let love into your heart and allow it to heal you.

Open your mind to the possibility and potential that love is already present within your life, resides within your body, and exists within your mind and soul. Since love has permeated all things, it goes to reason that love is within you, within your heart, your memories, your present, your future, and every aspect of who you are. You are literally the byproduct of love in its purest form so why keep going on through life thinking you are unloved and feeling unconfident? This simply cannot be possible as you are the result of love. I did not get into this profound understanding of love until I was deep into my personal discovery journey when I was in my late thirties, but it taught me to be kinder to myself, to love myself more, and to remember how powerful I actually am. There is no need to go out and find love elsewhere when love is already who you are. When I realized this profound truth, I finally understood my worth and my full valuation of myself. If I already was love and was made from love than why would I believe for a moment that I was unworthy of love?

This is why love is the most powerful force in the universe. It exists within everything and when you come to understand this as fact, you begin to see that there is no room for any hate within your heart. Love conquers all because love is within all. When you come to this conclusion, you will understand that there is no separation, there is only unity. Through love and unity, we realize our differences are only superficial and skin deep and any change within us is possible. All the potential that has ever existed resides within you now, the power of change is inside your grasp and all that it takes is your action, effort, and self-belief. Believe that you are loved and make it possible for yourself to achieve something incredible by having the confidence that it already exists within you.

Love can also inspire us to become better people, as we strive to live up to the high expectations and standards that come with being in a loving relationship. Love also has the power to heal emotional wounds and bring a sense of peace and comfort to those who are hurting. When we experience love, whether it be through a romantic relationship, a friendship, or a family connection, we feel a sense of safety and security that can help us overcome difficult times. Love can help us cope with loss and grief and can bring a sense of hope and resilience to even the darkest moments. Love can inspire us, heal us, and connect us to others in a way that is truly transformative. Whether we are giving love or receiving it, we are constantly reminded of the power and beauty of this universal force.

Kindness

I believe in practicing kindness in all aspects of life and business. Since kindness is so close to my heart, I make conscious efforts to practice it daily. There were so many times in my life that I only wished and hoped that someone would show me kindness and I remember craving kindness but not receiving it. When you feel this way, the very best thing you can do is to show kindness to someone else. No matter how low you may feel, how the world is treating you or what condition you are in, there is always ample room to show kindness to others. An act of kindness, even a small one can impact someone else's life so never hold back on the kindness and compassion you show to others. While valuing kindness is important to display for others, it also means showing kindness to yourself. While kindness was always a priority for me and the way I treated others, until recently I hadn't thought of it as something that I could internalize for myself.

When I began to display kindness towards myself, I started to realize how I was talking to myself and what it was doing to me. I began to see that for years I had said nothing but negative things to myself, things that I would never say to someone else. Every time I began to say something unkind to myself such as "I'm fat," "I'm ugly," "I'm not smart enough," or anything of that sort I stopped myself and corrected myself to say the opposite. Instead of saying these very narrow and unkind things to myself I began to say growth-oriented things to myself and positive affirmations. Eventually with enough time and practice, the negative voices that were once dominate began to become dormant. It is simply not possible to become the most confident version of yourself if you are unkind to yourself and if you practice negative self-talk. A truly confident person is kind to themselves and others. Anyone who diminishes themselves, their worth or someone else's worth is not a kind or confident person. Chances are there are deep insecurities which exist within that person that surface in the form of bullying, gossiping, or hateful speech. The best thing you can do is to not surround yourself with people like this because we become like those who we are in proximity of.

Kindness is confidence and as you go through your journey of becoming more confident you will do well to avoid negativity and unkindness as much as you possibly can. This is one of the main reasons I realized that working in a toxic work environment under toxic leadership was no longer something I could do. It went against my top core values and was the opposite of everything I believed in. I could no longer watch as leadership belittled coworkers, myself, or others. I could no longer stand back and be idle as I watched and witnessed repeated offenses that went in direct opposition to kindness. It began to feel as though my being surrounded by this toxicity and unkindness at work that I was accepting it and permitting it somehow. The more I surrounded myself with negativity and with people who were unkind to themselves, the more I began to realize how it was impacting me and it became soul crushing. I could no longer stand it, I felt as if I wanted to crawl out of my skin. I remember being present in meetings where my CEO would belittle everyone from the President of the company down, all the while waiting to be next on his chopping block. I didn't want to live this way or work for a company or leadership that practiced unkindness so prolifically. This fear and profound unkindness stayed with me for a long time until I realized that it didn't have to be my reality. Once I decided to choose kindness and let it enter every aspect of my life it made the choice to leave negativity and toxicity behind very clear. You cannot choose kindness and be surrounded by its opposite, it simply will not work, and you will live a life feeling trapped, disingenuous, and unfulfilled.

Faith

For you to attain to your most confident version of yourself you need to have gratitude for the person you are becoming, this requires unwavering faith that it will be so. Faith is spiritual and profound, but it is more than just metaphysical, it can also be very physical. For example, when medical patients ingest placebo drugs, they take them with the faith that they will be effective and workout for them in their favor. The placebo effect is a phenomenon where a person experiences a perceived improvement in their condition after receiving a treatment that is inactive or has no therapeutic effect. The effect is typically attributed to the person's belief or expectation that the treatment will help them, rather than any active ingredient or mechanism in the treatment itself. In other words, the person's mind and belief in the treatment's efficacy can create a real, physical response in their body. Placebo effects have been observed in a wide range of conditions, from pain relief and anxiety to Parkinson's disease and depression.

Researchers believe that the placebo effect may involve

the release of natural painkillers and other neurotransmitters in the brain, as well as changes in the body's stress response (Wager T.D., and Atlas L.Y., 2015). The placebo effect is an important consideration in medical research, as it can influence the outcomes of clinical trials and the effectiveness of treatments. This faith helps the patient heal, even if that patient is receiving a placebo sugar pill instead of an actual prescription drug. Clearly, our bodies and minds have the capacity to heal themselves without prescriptive drugs and through faith. Since this power of healing exists within us already, it goes without saying that we have the power within ourselves to heal our past, form new beliefs, overcome mental barriers, and become the best possible versions of ourselves through faith.

Faith is more than just a belief something will work out; it is a system of practices that you need to have continual devotion to. However, when working towards a goal, it is important to have more than faith alone. Without corresponding action, it is not enough to bring about positive change in the world or to bring us closer to the divine. Faith, by its very nature, implies a belief or trust in something greater than ourselves. This belief can be a powerful force that motivates us to act in ways that align with our values and beliefs. However, without corresponding action, faith can become stagnant and ineffective. For example, if we have faith that we can make a difference in the world, but we do not act towards that goal, our faith may not result in any meaningful change. Similarly, if we have faith in a higher power, but we do not actively seek to connect with that power through prayer, meditation, or other spiritual practices, our faith may not lead to a deeper understanding or connection. On the other hand, when faith is accompanied by action, it can be a powerful force for good. When we act towards our goals, we demonstrate our commitment to our beliefs and values. In religious and spiritual contexts, faith without action can also be seen as hypocritical or insincere. If we claim to have faith in a particular belief system, but our actions do not align with those beliefs, our faith may not be taken seriously by others. Overall, the idea that faith without action is fruitless reminds us of the importance of aligning our beliefs with our actions. By taking action towards our goals and living in accordance with our values, we can create a more meaningful and fulfilling life, as well as contribute to positive change in the world. When you begin to have faith in yourself it lays the path possible to grow and develop confidence. Just as a placebo drug works physically within the body to bring about positive change, so does faith through acts of self-belief.

Have the faith that the most confident person you are becoming already exists within you. It is not necessary for you to become a completely different person for you to become confident, you simply need to have the faith that that person will be revealed through persistent action. Consider this to be your placebo drug for confidence. The amount of confidence you can achieve is proportionate to the amount of faith and self-belief that exists within you. However, remember that you only need to have a small spark and seed of faith and confidence that you are deserving of more for you to become more.

Impact

The only way you can create the level of impact you need to create in this world is by being unapologetically you.

There is no room for comparison when you are creating impact because there is no comparison when you are operating on a higher plane of existence, there is only awareness, not competition or comparison. You are doing yourself an extreme disservice by comparing yourself to other people, you were meant to stand out, you were meant to be seen and heard and be different. The only way you can accomplish this is by creating impact through authenticity and not diminishing yourself and lessen your worth by placing your value on someone else's identity. Your story, your struggle, your strife, your past and your turmoil have all been secretly working toward your purpose in monumental ways. There is no room for doubt when you are seeking impact. You must think of impact with the intention of helping others and the world around you. The analogy I use for impact is simple. If you are in the middle of a still lake and drop a small stone, it will create small ripples that eventually dissipate. These ripples become larger with the size of the stone. If you have a large enough stone than the impact will be so large that it may even reach the shores of the lake and be felt throughout. Any level of impact is important and can help change the world but the larger the amount of impact we create, the more lives we can change.

This is one of the main reasons I decided to take my coaching business to less of a one-on-one approach and more one-to-many approach. Through writing this book and speaking to audiences, I can create increased amounts of impact and help more people reach their goals. I would not be able to change as many lives as I needed by having a small approach, I knew I needed to amplify my voice to accomplish my goals for impact and change. When you value impact, it means that you deeply care about changing the world. You find it difficult to sit back and watch things as they are, you believe change is possible, and you want it for everyone. While I am a leader in many respects, I am a guide first. Through my lens, I see the world as something that can be changed, and I wish to convey this vision to all that I encounter.

At the end of my life, I would love to be able to say that I created impact so large that it was felt the world over and that I helped thousands of people or more achieve greater levels of fulfillment, confidence, and purpose with my messages. However, if I can help a handful of people or even reach one life, then I have created impact that is beyond myself. This is my goal; I am here on this Earth to share my story to help others achieve what they are fully capable of achieving. My purpose is to inspire you to become the best version of yourself and to give you the tools needed to create the impact you need to create to make the world a better place for all. This is the power of collective impact versus individual impact. While one small stone may create ripple effects on the lake when dropped, many stones dropped into the lake will create several ripples. Even though the stones may be small, together collectively they can work to achieve a similar result as one large stone can. Never underestimate the size or scale of the impact you create. Encourage others to pay it forward and when you help someone, encourage them to do the same for someone else in return. What starts off as small impact, can turn into massive amounts of change very quickly if everyone is working on the collective greater good.

Anyone can create impact, regardless of their background

or circumstances. Impact can be created in many ways, from small acts of kindness and generosity to larger-scale initiatives that address societal challenges. The key to creating impact is to identify a need or problem in the world and take action to address it. This might involve volunteering with a local organization, donating money or resources to a cause you care about, or starting your own initiative to tackle a particular issue. Impact can also be created through everyday actions, such as being kind to others, practicing sustainability, or advocating for causes you believe in. Every positive action we take has the potential to create a ripple effect, inspiring others to act which creates positive change in the world. It's important to remember that creating impact doesn't always require huge amounts of time, money, or resources. Even small actions can make a difference, and every effort counts. What's most important is that we are intentional and thoughtful in our actions, and that we are committed to making a positive difference in the world and within ourselves. Ultimately, creating impact requires a combination of passion, commitment, action, and deep purpose. By taking small steps every day to make a difference in your own life and in the lives of others, you can create a ripple effect of positive change that can have a lasting impact on the world around you.

One way to make a more significant impact is to focus on a specific issue that you are passionate about. By identifying a particular issue and focusing your efforts on that issue, you can make a more targeted and effective impact. This might involve working with a particular organization or group or using your skills and expertise to address a specific problem. By dedicating your time, energy, and resources to a specific issue, you can make a tangible difference in the lives of others.

Another way to create more impact is to build a network of like-minded individuals who share your values and vision. By connecting with others who are passionate about the same issues as you, you can amplify your impact and create a movement for change. This might involve connecting with others through social media, attending events and conferences, or joining existing groups and organizations. By working together and sharing resources and expertise, you can achieve greater impact than you would be able to achieve alone.

Using technology to your advantage is also a great way to create more impact. In today's digital age, technology can be a powerful tool for creating change. By using social media, online fundraising platforms, and other digital tools, you can reach a larger audience and mobilize support for your cause. For example, crowdfunding platforms such as Kickstarter or GoFundMe can help raise funds for a specific project or initiative, while social media platforms can help spread awareness and mobilize support for your cause. Ultimately, creating significant impact requires determination, persistence, and a willingness to take risks and think creatively but if impact is one of your core values you will find a way to make it happen. For me, impact means guiding people to see their potential, loving, and supporting them without judgment, taking my message to a large scale, and helping people overcome their limitations. If I can impact the world with my messages, I will absolutely do it but ultimately if I can change at least one life than I have accomplished my mission to create impact. All I ask in return is that anyone

I help do the same for someone else and pay it forward.

Freedom

Freedom as a core value is about valuing individual autonomy and the ability to make choices and pursue your own goals and dreams. By embracing freedom as a core value, individuals can strive to live their lives in a way that aligns with their values and promotes greater freedom and opportunity for all. Through freedom we get the opportunity to experience life to a fuller extent and can choose how and who we spend our lives with. For me, freedom was about working when I wanted to work, be with my family as much as I could, and not be confined to someone else's version of what I should be.

For years of my young adult life, I was employed in a corporate workplace living and working on someone's else's dream and towards someone else's version of success. I remember thinking to myself that if I just worked harder, if I just got promoted, if I just made more money, if I just got a new title, I would be happy. I kept chasing an idea of someone else's version of success, all the while not realizing that it was not aligned with what I wanted out of life. Once I left my corporate job and decided to venture out into entrepreneurship full-time, I began to understand how much I valued freedom, and this helped guide and steer my choices.

When I started thinking about what I wanted out of life instead of focusing on what I didn't want it changed everything for me and made choices and decisions crystal clear. Prior to deciding to become a full-time entrepreneur I was offered a position to run a division at a fortune 500 company Headquartered in Tennessee. The position would have represented a 30% increase in my base salary plus much more opportunities for income with commission. My family and I were preparing to move. We began having serious talks about moving out of state, switching school systems for our daughter, picking out houses and neighborhoods and going through all the motions to make a big move. I kept picking different models of homes or different lots or different neighborhoods and each time they inexplicably fell through. It was as if some unseen force was working against my every action and plan to move. I remember feeling as though the whole experience was a failure, I got offered what I thought would be my dream job and I failed to secure a home that would get me there. I didn't understand why I kept failing and couldn't comprehend why nothing seemed to work out. However, it wasn't just me who was failing. My husband also was failing to secure a full-time job in the area and for us to make the move to a more expensive city, we both needed steady incomes.

There were so many things that kept getting in the way until I realized something very powerful. There was an unseen force that was preventing me from making that move and while I don't have all the words to express it, I know that it was happening. It was too coincidental for it not to be the case to the point where it felt as if the Universe itself was conspiring against it. After going from several toxic workplaces one right after the other and working towards someone else's dream for so long there was no way I could go back to the way it was and expect a different outcome. I realized that the reason why I was failing was because the move would have resulted in a potentially larger failure. There was a force that was working to prevent me from a greater failure and ultimately saved my family and myself. I am convinced that if we were to have moved and changed jobs that I would not be writing this book today, I may not be alive at all. At this point in my life, I was battling severe depression and contemplating suicide, so I strongly feel that something was preventing me from the move to avoid this disastrous consequence.

I realized that any failure is simply redirection and that these perceived failures that come into our lives are not actually failures at all but rather lessons. Once I identified freedom as something that I valued highly and something I truly wanted out of life it became painfully obvious that I could no longer be a cog in the machine, I knew that I had to step outside of my comfort zone and do something incredible. I knew I had to make the change and believe in myself to have the life I wanted. I knew the life I wanted was within my grasp if I lived it on my own terms, not anyone else's. We made the decision to stay where we were and for me to try full-time entrepreneurship and to take a leap of faith and trust in myself.

Even though entrepreneurship aligned with my values and what I wanted, it was far from easy. After leaving my corporate job I lost my company car, company cell phone, company computer, and no longer got reimbursed for travel expenses. I was on my own and it was a bit terrifying. I also didn't have life, dental, or health insurance and being a mother of a young family that was risky. The last thing I needed to have happen was an accident or a trip to the hospital that I couldn't afford. I was willing to give it all up for the ability to work on my own dream in my own terms, but I had nothing when I started. My laptop that I did have was old and everything possible started going wrong with it. The screen started to yellow and warp, the battery started to swell up and my camera was not great. On top of this I didn't have a car and at the age of 38 I was borrowing my mother's car. In many respects on the surface, it seemed as if I was failing but inside, I felt driven, confident in my abilities to overcome, and purposeful. As a wife and mom, I also had to think about balancing work and my personal life. I knew if I didn't create some type of balance and have personal freedom, it could lead to depression, anxiety of lack of fulfillment again.

On the outside, it looked like I was failing but, on the

inside, I was finally experiencing freedom for the first time in my life, and I was loving it. To be able to make my own schedule, do work that I loved, and live on my own terms was something so exciting to me that any risk that I had to make seemed worth it. Since I started embracing freedom more and more, I began to realize that there was no going back, for me to feel fulfilled, happy, purposeful, and confident, I needed to be my own boss and run my own company.

I do want to emphasize that it is possible to value freedom and still work for someone else. Valuing freedom can mean different things to different people and doesn't necessarily mean that one needs to be self-employed or run their own business. For some people, freedom might mean having flexibility in their work schedule or being able to work from home. For others, it might mean having autonomy and control over their work projects or being able to pursue their own interests and passions within their job. Working for someone else doesn't necessarily mean giving up these freedoms. Many companies and organizations offer flexible work arrangements, and some even prioritize employee autonomy and empowerment. It's also possible to negotiate for these types of freedoms within a job, and to find ways to incorporate your own interests and passions into your work. Ultimately, whether working for someone else aligns with your values around freedom depends on your individual circumstances and priorities. It's important to reflect on what freedom means to you, and to explore ways to incorporate those values into your work and daily life.

It can sometimes be challenging to identify exactly what you want out of life, not everyone has a clearly defined path that they have always known. However, the best thing you can do in any scenario is to stop settling for less than you deserve, stop settling for things that do not serve you, and stop settling for things that make you unhappy and less confident. Life is not worth living if you are surrounded by an environment which makes you feel unsatisfied, depressed, unconfident, or anxious. No amount of money will ever make up for a lack of purpose. Even if we are financially successful, we may still feel a sense of emptiness or dissatisfaction if we are not doing work that truly matters to us that aligns with our values.

When we step into the realm of purpose, we tap into a wellspring of profound fulfillment, joy, and significance. It is a place where our unique talents harmonize with our deepest values, and our actions ripple outwards, touching the lives of others and leaving an indelible mark on the world. Each day becomes a canvas on which we paint our purpose, infusing every moment with intention, passion, and unwavering commitment. When we align with our purpose, every step becomes infused with meaning, every challenge transforms into an opportunity for growth, and every decision is guided by our inner compass. It is in these moments that we witness the extraordinary unfold—the limitless possibilities, the profound connections, and the sheer joy that radiates from within. Embrace your purpose and unleash your unstoppable confidence, for within it lies the transformative power to illuminate your path and radiate your truest potential to the world.

Practice these positive affirmations to stay mindful of your purpose. Say them as many times as necessary to remind yourself that you are an infinite being and that you were created with love and divine purpose:

1. I have a unique purpose and calling in life, and I am grateful for the opportunity to fulfill it.
2. I am aligned with my higher purpose, and I trust that everything is unfolding for my highest good.
3. I am committed to discovering my true calling and using my gifts, talents, and story to make a positive impact in the world.
4. I am in tune with my inner guidance and intuition, which leads me towards my purpose and highest potential.
5. I am grateful for the clarity and insight that comes from living in alignment with my purpose and higher calling.
6. I am open to new opportunities and experiences that align with my purpose and help me fulfill my higher calling.
7. I am dedicated to using my talents and skills to serve others and make a positive difference in the world.
8. I am confident in my ability to fulfill my purpose and live a meaningful life.

9. I am grateful for the challenges and obstacles that help me grow and develop in my journey towards fulfilling my purpose and higher calling.
10. I am focused on living a purpose-driven life and using my unique gifts and talents to create a better world for myself and others.

Takeaways from this Chapter:

- *Identify Your Core Values:* Discovering your purpose begins with identifying your core values – the deeply held beliefs and principles that guide your life. Reflect on what matters most to you, and let these values serve as the foundation for your purpose.

- *Create a Value-Based Vision:* Craft a vision for your life that aligns with your core values. Envision how your values can manifest in your daily actions, relationships, and contributions to the world.

- *Prioritize Meaning Over Materialism:* Pursuing a purpose aligned with your core values shifts your focus from material possessions to meaningful experiences and impact. Prioritize fulfillment and growth over the pursuit of external validation.

- *Integrate Values into Decision Making:* Use your core values as a compass when making decisions. Consider whether choices align with your values and let them guide you toward the path that resonates with your purpose.

- *Embrace Authenticity:* Living in harmony with your core values allows you to be authentic and true to yourself. Embrace your uniqueness, and let your values shape your identity and actions.

- *Seek Purposeful Opportunities:* Purpose-driven individuals actively seek opportunities that align with their values. Look for avenues to express your core beliefs through meaningful work, volunteer activities, or personal projects.

- *Overcome Obstacles with Values:* When faced with challenges, rely on your core values for strength and resilience. Let them inspire you to persevere and find creative solutions that stay true to your purpose.

- *Review & Realign:* Regularly review your core values and purpose. As you grow and evolve, your values might shift, and your purpose may take on new dimensions. Embrace change and realign your life accordingly.

Lessons Learned from Finding Your Purpose through Core Values:

- *Meaningful Direction:* Discovering your purpose through core values provides a clear and meaningful direction for your life. Your values become a guiding force, steering you toward fulfillment and significance.
- *Anchoring in Turbulent Times:* Core values serve as anchors during turbulent times. When life feels uncertain, your values keep you grounded and focused on what truly matters.
- *Authenticity & Integrity:* Living in alignment with your core values enhances your authenticity and integrity. You become a person of conviction, reflecting your beliefs in all aspects of your life.
- *Greater Resilience:* Purpose found in core values empowers you to bounce back from setbacks with greater resilience. Your values provide a source of strength,

enabling you to face challenges head-on.

- *Deeper Connection:* Embracing your purpose through core values fosters deeper connections with others who share similar beliefs. You attract like-minded individuals and form meaningful relationships.
- *Inner Fulfillment:* Living a purpose-driven life based on core values brings profound inner fulfillment and contentment. You experience a sense of harmony within yourself and with the world around you.
- *Legacy of Impact:* Purpose aligned with core values allows you to leave a meaningful legacy. Your actions and contributions ripple beyond your lifetime, influencing others and making a positive impact.

Why It Is Important:

Finding your purpose through your core values is a transformative process that brings immense significance to your life. It ensures that your actions and decisions are rooted in what truly matters to you, leading to a life of authenticity and fulfillment.

When you align with your core values, your purpose becomes a guiding light, illuminating your path even in challenging times. You draw strength from your values, allowing you to overcome obstacles and persevere with unwavering resolve.

Living in harmony with your core values creates a deep sense of purpose, anchoring you to a life of meaning and impact. Embrace the power of your core values as you navigate through life and let them lead you to a purposeful journey filled with authenticity, connection, and fulfillment.

Your Turn:

1.) What are your top 3-5 core values and why are they important to you?

2.) Are you currently living aligned with your core values?
Yes or No

3.) What action steps can you take today to live a life that is aligned with your core values?

4.) What needs to be removed from your life to align with your core values?

5.) What needs to be added in your life to align with your core values?

Conclusion

The method for developing confidence that is outlined in this book is attainable for anyone to achieve. Gratitude, Responsibility, Action, Sight, and Purpose are all essential components of a confident and fulfilling life. Each of these elements contributes to building a sense of self-worth, which in turn can lead to increased confidence. Practicing gratitude can help you develop a positive outlook on life, which can contribute to greater confidence. When you focus on the good things in your life and express appreciation for them, you cultivate a sense of abundance and contentment. This can help you feel more grounded and secure in who you are, which can boost your confidence. Taking responsibility for your actions, mindset, and decisions is another important factor in building confidence. When you own up to your mistakes and failures and take steps to correct them, you demonstrate a sense of accountability and maturity. This can help you feel more in control of your life and more confident in your ability to handle challenges. Acting towards your goals and dreams is a critical component of confidence-building. When you take concrete steps towards what you want in life, you demonstrate a commitment to your own success. Each step you take, no matter how small, builds momentum and contributes to a sense of progress and achievement. This can help you feel more capable and self-assured. Having a clear vision and sight of what you want out of life is also important for building confidence. When you have a sense of direction and a clarity of vision, you have something to strive for which can help you feel more motivated and energized. Purpose can help you feel more confident in your decisions and actions, as you are working towards something meaningful and fulfilling.

These five simple steps: **G**ratitude, **R**esponsibility, **A**ction, **S**ight, and **P**urpose changed my life in more ways than one. These steps didn't require me to learn new skills or develop talents and failure was simply not possible. Once I understood that the foundation to confidence was gratitude, that I oversaw my future, that my past was a lesson-not a life sentence, that my mindset created my reality, that my vision was essential for me to progress towards my goals, and that

I had a divine purpose and calling I began to become more confident and so will you.

What started as a small unformed seed of faith that I could become confident, eventually became a process that I began to trust and live by. Even after I began to have faith in a higher calling and purpose as well as faith in myself there was still a missing element that took me time to fully capture and understand. This element was faith in divine timing. Divine timing is the belief that everything in the universe happens according to a higher plan or purpose, and that events unfold at the perfect time, orchestrated by a higher power or force. It is the idea that there is a divine or spiritual timing that governs the unfolding of events in our lives, rather than things happening purely by chance or coincidence. Those who believe in divine timing believe that everything happens for a reason, and that every experience, whether positive or negative, is necessary for our growth and spiritual evolution. They believe that when we trust in the divine timing of events, we can let go of our need for control and surrender to the unfolding of life. At the same time, this belief in divine timing doesn't mean that we should sit back and wait for things to happen to us. Rather, it is about taking action and doing our part to create the life we want, while also trusting through faith that the universe will guide us towards the right opportunities and experiences at the right time.

As someone who is ambitious and a high achiever, I normally can be quite impatient when I begin to go after my goals. I generally like to go after something very hard until I get it and I tend to get frustrated when something does not happen quickly. Through my journey I began to realize that this was not how the universe worked. While you will get achievements and progress along the way, you must learn lessons and experience setbacks to fully step into your purpose and best version of yourself. There are things you must learn and experience along the way that help you become who you are supposed to be. Through divine timing I began to realize that I needed to have greater faith that every failure and setback was a part of my process and journey and that no amount of impatience was getting me closer to my goals. Impatience can lead to you giving up on your goals because you feel as though things are not happening soon enough. Trust the process and simply let go of the outcome. By letting go of the outcome and by trusting the process you are having faith and if you do this enough, everything you want will come to fruition for you. You must accept that your timeline is a construct of your ego and may not align with God's plan for you. Keep walking in your faith, keep trusting that everything will happen at the perfect time, and keep believing that you are already well on your way to reach your goals.

Through daily self-work and mindfulness practices I began to see my way out of the dark cave I was in. I started to see things as they could be instead of just accepting them as they were. I started to stand up for myself more, say no to things that did not serve me, and say yes to myself more. I went from putting myself last to putting myself first and every cell in my body began to feel the positive effects of my actions. The depression and anxiety that were once prevalent in my life began to be a thing of the past until they dissipated completely. The things I used to fear began to be the things that excited me the most. I started to love myself and as I write this, I cannot be more grateful for how far I have come in my journey. Gratitude, Responsibility, Action, Sight, and Purpose all play a crucial role in building confidence. By cultivating these qualities, you can develop a strong sense of self-worth which can help you feel more confident in yourself and your abilities. Think, believe, and achieve in becoming the person you were always meant to be and start with the knowledge that that person already exists within you. The confident person who you envisioned yourself to be in the previous chapters is eagerly awaiting to be revealed to the world. Within each passing moment, that person is cheering you on and wishing for your success.

The time to change your life begins now and it is imperative that your actions from this moment on are with a sense of urgency. Our time is not promised, and tomorrow is not guaranteed to any of us. Therefore, for you to live to your purpose and attain confidence you need to act now. Your life begins the moment you unleash your confidence and step into your power. Stop waiting for permission and start acting. You are the exact remedy for an ailment that exists within the world, but it requires a higher version of yourself for you to achieve this purpose. The world needs you; the divine has assigned you, your time is now. GRASP confidence and own your power!

Key Takeaways from this Book:

- *Embrace Gratitude:* Gratitude is the key that unlocks the door to your most successful and confident self. Recognize the abundance in your life and cultivate appreciation for your achievements and experiences, no matter how big or small.
- *Adopt a Responsibility Mindset:* Take ownership of your life and decisions. Embrace responsibility for your actions, choices, and outcomes. A responsibility mindset empowers you to create your own path to success and confidently navigate through challenges.
- *Take Inspired Action:* Combine your vision with proactive steps towards your goals. Through consistent and inspired action, you turn dreams into reality and steadily progress towards becoming the person you aspire to be.
- *Keep Your Sights Clear:* Visualize your most successful

and confident self regularly. See yourself living your vision, overcoming obstacles, and enjoying the fruits of your labor. Clear sights fuel determination and belief in your potential.

- *Discover Your Purpose & Align With It:* Uncover your life's purpose by aligning with your core values and deepest beliefs. Your purpose gives direction and meaning to your journey, guiding you towards fulfillment and success.

Lessons Learned from Becoming Your Most Successful and Confident Self:

- *You Are Already That Person Within:* Know that your most successful and confident self already resides within you. You possess the strength, capabilities, and potential to achieve greatness.
- *Gratitude Nurtures Growth:* Gratitude is the fertile soil in which confidence and success thrive. By appreciating your journey and the lessons learned, you create a positive mindset that fuels further growth.
- *Confidence Fuels Achievement:* Confidence is both

a catalyst and a result of achievement. As you take action and achieve small wins, your confidence grows, propelling you to aim higher and achieve even more.

- *Responsibility Drives Empowerment:* Embracing responsibility for your life empowers you to shape your future. It reinforces that you have the power to make choices and create outcomes that align with your vision.
- *Purpose Magnifies Impact:* Discovering your purpose connects your goals to a higher calling. Purpose-driven actions have a more profound impact on both your life and the lives of others, as they align with your deepest values
- *You Control Your Destiny:* You hold the pen to your life's narrative. Through gratitude, a responsibility mindset, inspired action, clear sights, and purpose, you can write a story of success, confidence, and fulfillment.
- *Transformation Is a Journey:* Becoming your most successful and confident self is a continuous journey, not a destination. Embrace the process, celebrate each milestone, and remain open to growth and learning.

Your Turn:

1.) What are your biggest takeaways from this book and lessons learned?

2.) What action steps are you willing to do today and for the rest of your life to make Gratitude, Responsibility, Action, Sight, and Purpose a daily habit and choice?

3.) Who or what do you need to remove from your life to become unstoppably confident?

About the Author

Tara is a CEO, keynote speaker, author, and chairwoman, and coach. She holds an MBA with a specialization in Business Analytics from the University of North Carolina at Wilmington as well as certifications from Cornell University in Financial Management and The University of Notre Dame in Management. Additionally, Tara is the United States Country Chair for Startup Ecosystems for the G100 Mission Million, a global women's leadership network. Her role as Country Chair is to appoint and support female entrepreneurs within every State and provide them with networking opportunities and knowledge that enable them to grow and scale their businesses. In 2024 Tara will have the honor of speaking on the TEDx stage in Nottinghamshire, England teaching gratitude as the foundation for confidence from lessons taught in this book.

Tara lives in central North Carolina with her husband, daughter, and family dogs. She enjoys nature, spending time with her family, traveling, going to the beach, gardening, cooking, and baking. As a speaker, she is passionate about teaching and loves nurturing her audiences with her inspiring and uplifting messages that positively impact their lives. As a leader, she seeks to show people what is possible for them, regardless of the adversity they have faced in their life. Tara's mission is to leave a legacy behind that remains long after she is gone, and she wants to do this through love, authenticity, kindness and by sharing her story with the world.

Special Acknowledgements

To my dear friends and colleagues who I entrusted to read my book prior to publishing made all the difference in bringing this book to life in a meaningful way. Thank you for your support and weekly contributions, you helped my book come to life fully and wonderfully.

Lina Echeverry-Hart- My dear friend, thank you so much for believing in me and encouraging me to soar continually to new heights and pursue my dreams. Our weekly calls make all the difference in the level of motivation I have; without your continual support I wouldn't be where I am today. I am truly grateful for our friendship, you genuinely want the best for me, and it shows with every action you take. Thank you for always being in my corner.

Mitzie Williams- God brought us together and made our connection possible. I am so grateful to have you in my life, and for the bond we share. Thank you for giving me the opportunity of a lifetime by inviting me to become a speaker on your stage. You completely transformed my life by believing in my idea, my message, and who I am as a person. Words cannot express the amount of gratitude that fills my heart every time I think about you, what you have done, and continue to do to help me. We share the same values and beliefs, and I couldn't ask for a more wonderful person to work with, learn from, and be mentored by.

Cindi Cohn- Thank you so much for supporting me and believing in me but most importantly, having faith in me. You never once doubted in me or my abilities to become an author or speaker. You helped me secure my first television interview and you guided me to success and accomplishing major life-changing goals. Thank you for your kindness and for openly and lovingly sharing your experience, time, and resources with me. Its friends like you that make it possible to level up in life.

Gary B. Doherty- You were the first person to ever tell me I had a TED worthy idea. You looked in my eyes and believed in me and then helped me accomplish my wildest dreams. I am so thankful that we met and decided to work together. You elevated me and showed support and encouragement all along the way. I am so grateful for having you in my life.

Citations

Lambersky, S. (2013) https://financialpost.com/entrepreneur/three-techniques-to-manage-40000-negative-thoughts#:~:text=We%20produce%20up%20to%2050%2C000,for%20any%20person%20or%20entrepreneur., How to manage your 40,000 negative thoughts a day and keep moving forward. Available at: https://financialpost.com/entrepreneur/three-techniques-to-manage-40000-negative-thoughts (Accessed: 21 July 2023).

Associates N., (2022) Gratitude literally rewires your brain to be happier, NeuroHealth Associates. Available at: https://nhahealth.com/neuroscience-reveals-gratitude-literally-rewires-your-brain-to-be-happier/ (Accessed: 30 June 2023). Clance, P. R., & Imes, S. A. (1978). The imposter phenomenon in high achieving women: Dynamics and therapeutic intervention. Psychotherapy: Theory, Research & Practice, 15(3), 241–247. https://doi.org/10.1037/h0086006

Elting L., (2023) New Year, New Glass Heights: Women now comprise 10% of top U.S. corporation CEOS, Forbes. Available at: https://www.forbes.com/sites/lizelting/2023/01/27/new-year-new-glass-heights-for-the-first-time-in-history-over-10-of-fortune-500-ceos-are-women/?sh=166ff8b3e77f (Accessed: 01 July 2023).

Gardner,E.L., (2011) Addiction and brain reward and Antireward Pathways, Advances in psychosomatic medicine. Available at: https://www.ncbi.nlm.nih.gov/pmc/articles/PMC4549070/ (Accessed: 30 June 2023).

Hair NL, Hanson JL, Wolfe BL, Pollak SD. Association of Child Poverty, Brain Development, and Academic Achievement. JAMA Pediatr. 2015;169(9):822–829. doi:10.1001/jamapediatrics.2015.1475 Lechner, T.

How much of communication is nonverbal?: UT permian basin online (2023) UTPB. Available at: https://online.utpb.edu/about-us/articles/communication/how-much-of-communication-is-nonverbal/ (Accessed: 01 July 2023).

(2022) The neuroscience behind gratitude: How does cultivating appreciation affect your brain?, Chopra. Available at: https://chopra.com/articles/the-neuroscience-behind-gratitude-how-does-cultivating-appreciation-affect-your-brain#:~:text=A%20recent%20study%20found%20that,craves%20the%20experience%20of%20giving. (Accessed: 30 June 2023).

(2022) Princetonhcs.org. Available at: https://www.princetonhcs.org/about-princeton-health/news-and-information/news/can-gratitude-increase-quality-of-life#:~:text=%E2%80%94When%20gratitude%20is%20expressed%20and,%2C%20and%20overall%20well%2D-being. (Accessed: 30 June 2023).

(No date) Stress and the developing brain - ECMHC. Available at: https://www.ecmhc.org/tutorials/trauma/mod2_3.html (Accessed: 30 June 2023).

Wager, T.D. and Atlas, L.Y. (2015) The neuroscience of placebo effects: Connecting context, learning and health, Nature reviews. Neuroscience. Available at: https://www.ncbi.nlm.nih.gov/pmc/articles/PMC6013051/ (Accessed: 01 July 2023).

Contact:

Tara LaFon Gooch, MBA

Website: www.taralafongooch.com

Social Media: @taralafongooch

Made in the USA
Middletown, DE
12 August 2023

36534267R00163